A BRIEF HISTORY OF

WITCHCRAFT

LOIS
MARTIN

RUNNING PRESS
PHILADELPHIA · LONDON

ROBINSON

Constable & Robinson Ltd
3 The Lanchesters
162 Fulham Palace Road
London W6 9ER
www.constablerobinson.com

First published in the UK by Robinson,
an imprint of Constable & Robinson, 2010

A copy of the British Library Cataloguing in Publication Data
is available from the British Library

UK ISBN 978-1-84901-383-3

1 3 5 7 9 10 8 6 4 2

First published in the United States in 2010 by Running Press Book Publishers

US Library of Congress Control Number: 2009943293
US ISBN 978-0-7624-3989-8

Running Press Book Publishers
2300 Chestnut Street
Philadelphia, PA 19103-4371
Visit us on the web!
www.runningpress.com

Typeset by TW Typesetting, Plymouth, Devon
Printed and bound in the EU

CONTENTS

For Dad

INTRODUCTION

Harry Potter is in the ascendant and Wicca is one of the fastest-growing religions in the world today; in the twenty-first century witches and witchcraft still have us under a timeless magical spell. Harry Potter's phenomenal success owes much to author J.K. Rowling's masterful ability to bring to life some powerful archetypal figures. The witch, the wizard, the magician; we all intuitively know who they are and what they can do. Transformers, shape-shifters, healers, soothsayers, challengers, destroyers; every culture has its witches and wizards and in every culture they are both admired and feared. Young Harry Potter and his school friends neatly sum up the Western fairytale vision of the witch and the wizard. They fly on broomsticks, wear pointy hats, cast spells with magic wands, brew up potions in cauldrons, refer to dusty *grimoires* of magical instruction, and keep toads and owls as helpful familiars. To board the

Hogwarts Express is to leave reality far behind and to enter a world of fairytale dreamscapes and collective imagining, in which good and evil become a question of black and white and no one stops to ask how witches and wizards came to possess their awesome supernatural abilities.

Back in the real world, however, it is just such questions of good and evil, of natural and supernatural, which have long been at the core of our perceptions of witchcraft, and have shaped the role of witches and witchcraft in our society, often with deadly consequences. This Brief History looks at the relationship between the witch and society in European history. It is time-bound, geography-bound, and, most importantly, reality-bound. It does not deal with fairytale witchcraft, modern pagan witchcraft or witchcraft in non-European cultures. That said, to avoid misunderstanding and confusion, we should perhaps stop for a moment and define exactly what we mean by historical witchcraft and, in particular, how it differs from the modern pagan religion of Wicca. There have been many misconceptions amongst modern pagan witches about the origins of their faith and its relationship to the witchcraft of history. Recently, the scholar Ronald Hutton, in his book *The Triumph of the Moon*, has undertaken the first professional historical analysis of the birth of what he calls 'the only religion England has ever given the world', and Wicca has finally been given a firm historical foundation on which to rest, one based on sound academic principles and not on half-truths and romantic myth.

Perhaps the easiest way to approach the confusion and discrepancies that exist between modern pagan witchcraft and historical witchcraft is to look at the subject in terms of the two classical systems of thought that underpin each type of witchcraft. Whilst the magical element of Wicca is ultimately a child (or at least a great-great-great-great-grandchild) of the Neo-Platonic Renaissance, historical witchcraft beliefs had their foundations in medieval Aristotelian thought. The Aristotelian scholars of the Middle Ages believed that magic could only be performed with the aid of demons, hence the accusation that all witchcraft was the work of the Devil. The Renaissance thinkers, however, postulated that magic was a natural science and that absolutely no demons were necessary in order for humans to relate magically to their environment. Whilst Neo-Platonism posited a natural explanation for magic, Aristotelianism posited a supernatural explanation.

The Neo-Platonic system of thought became the dominant one amongst occultists who, since the Renaissance, have largely viewed the practice of magic in Neo-Platonic terms as an entirely natural phenomenon. In modern Wicca this Neo-Platonic occult philosophy of Natural Magic has found a bedfellow in the pantheistic pagan spirituality born out of the eighteenth-century Romantic movement. Wicca has given structure to a religious impulse that animates and imbues the whole of the natural world with a vital life force that moves in cycles of both generation and destruction and permeates and connects every living being. Gods, goddesses, faeries and spirits are viewed either as personifications of this holistic life force or as non-material entities arising from nature. There is no particular concept of good and evil, and man-made evils are generally seen as the result of alienation from nature and the life force that sustains it.

This witchcraft is a whole world (and system of thought) away from the witchcraft that began to take shape under the dominant Aristotelian worldview of the Christian Middle Ages and eventually settled into its classic stereotypical form towards the end of the fifteenth century. It is this view of witchcraft with which we will concern ourselves throughout the rest of this book. In this view, the witch was believed to make a pact with the Devil, whom she worshipped at nocturnal gatherings known as the Sabbat (or Sabbath), which usually took place in some wild and remote area or cave. She flew to the Sabbat with her fellow witches, usually on a broomstick, and there they paid homage to the Devil, whom they worshipped. They invoked demons, cooked up gruesome feasts consisting largely of the flesh of unbaptised babies, and then extinguished the lights and copulated indiscriminately with whomever was closest to hand. The Devil himself, or one of his lesser demons, presided over these Sabbats, and he usually appeared in the form of a man described as being black or dressed in black. At other times he appeared in the form of a goat, a dog, a cat, a toad, or some other animal. The Devil baptised his witches with a special identifying mark, known as the Devil's Mark, and they served him by committing various acts of *maleficia*, malicious and harmful sorcery, which usually took the form of bewitching their neighbours' cattle or children, blasting crops, and causing illness and death in their local communities. The witches gained their magical abilities from the Devil and were often aided in their destructive work by demons, who frequently took the form of familiars, or magical pets.

Whilst the ideological foundations for this witchcraft lie in the Middle Ages, it was not a medieval invention. It occurs both before and after the medieval era. Belief in witchcraft can be traced back into antiquity and the widespread persecution of witches popularly known as the Witch Craze did not get under way in earnest until the sixteenth and seventeenth centuries. Most of us are familiar with the so-called 'Burning Times', in which those accused of witchcraft were tortured and burnt at the stake. The seemingly epidemic proportions of these executions has led to the term 'craze' being applied to these outbreaks of witch-hunting, which appear to the modern observer to have been the result of some form of mass hysteria. To a large extent, the Witch Craze was a Western European phenomenon and witchcraft developed very differently in Western Europe than it did in Britain and the peripheral regions of Europe. In fact, the main force of the Witch Craze was concentrated within a relatively small central band of Western Europe encompassing France and Germany. The historian Robert Thurston has observed that 'one could draw a circle with a 300-mile radius around Strasbourg that would encompass well over 50 per cent of all witch trials'.

Historians have long sought to explain why the Witch Craze took place when and where it did. It is a phenomenon peculiar to a particular moment in European history, yet the belief in witchcraft was nothing new, and certainly not limited to Europe. The historical study of witchcraft has focused primarily on piecing together the many elements of European witch beliefs that ultimately combined to cause the deaths of an estimated 40,000 people for the alleged 'crime' of witchcraft during the Witch Craze. Many functional theories have been put forward to try to explain the Witch Craze, from social, economic and religious strife to the oppression of women and the need to find scapegoats on whom to blame misfortunes and natural disasters. While all these theories have a valid role to play in understanding the many factors that contributed to both the rise of witch-hunting in general and individual witch-hunts in particular, none of them satisfactorily explains the entire phenomenon. There is no 'one size fits all' theory that adequately covers the history of European witchcraft. Modern historians have concentrated on examining the relationships between the many cultural, religious and legal strands that gradually accumulated and evolved throughout the Middle Ages and into the early modern period and that created the unique set of conditions which allowed the Witch Craze to find form. Both the classic stereotype of the witch that developed on the Continent and the Devil she was alleged to serve were composite figures drawn from a number of different ideological and cultural sources, and fed by a variety of changes in the legal and social make-up of European society over a number of centuries. The belief in witchcraft did not fully exist in its classic, stereotypical form until the end of the fifteenth century, and it is to the preceding centuries that historians must look in order to unearth the origins of the witch beliefs that laid the foundations for the Witch Craze.

Witches and witchcraft have always been present in society in one form or another. In early medieval Europe common sorcerers and cunning folk were largely tolerated as part of the social fabric of daily life. Most jurisdictions had laws against using magic to inflict harm or cause death but prosecutions were not widespread. By the late medieval period and into the early modern period, however, witchcraft had taken on a very new and distinct meaning. The causes for this change in perception were mainly rooted in a new paranoia that was shaking the foundations of European society. Between the years 1000 and 1400 Europe underwent a major transformation in its social and political outlook. The military threat posed by invading Muslim armies, the split with the eastern Orthodox Church, the rise of heresy and the devastating arrival of the Black Death all combined to create a new siege mentality in the European psyche that would radically alter many aspects of social, spiritual and political life. Medieval Europe perceived itself as under attack and the later Middle Ages were overflowing with conspiracy theories; Jews, lepers, heretics and infidels were all targeted as the new 'enemies from within', plotting to destroy European Christendom in a diabolical conspiracy engineered by Satan himself. Gradually the figure of the witch began to emerge as the ultimate symbol of this covert evil working against society from within and the paranoia of the Middle Ages was carried over into the early modern period, sustained and propelled by a deep-seated fear of the Devil.

In this Brief History we will take a look at the origins of some of the ideological, cultural and legal developments that led to the formation of Continental European witch beliefs and analyse the main components of the classic witchcraft stereotype. We will also examine witch beliefs in the English-speaking world and how they differed from those on the Continent. We will conclude by taking a look at some of the theories that have attempted to answer the question of whether or not an actual witch cult ever really existed.

I

A BRIEF GUIDE TO THE DEVIL
AND ALL HIS WORKS

At the very heart of historical witchcraft beliefs lies the ominous figure of the Devil. Despite the increasing secularisation of much of Western culture the Devil is still firmly ingrained in our imaginations. We all think we know who the Devil is. He is Satan, the Prince of Darkness, author of all evil, also known as Lucifer, Beelzebub and many other names. He has horns, cloven hooves and a tail, and carries a pitchfork. He delights in leading sinners astray and ensnaring souls. His abode is the fiery pits of Hell and he commands vast legions of demons. But our ideas about the Devil are actually the conflation of a number of different influences that gradually merged and became more powerful and distinct during the course of the Middle Ages.

Unravelling the Threads

> And the great dragon was cast out, that old serpent,
> called the Devil, and Satan, which deceiveth the whole
> world: he was cast out into the earth, and his angels were
> cast out with him. (Revelations 12:9)

The singular concept of the Devil that emerged during
the Middle Ages was a synthesis of various Biblical and
mythical figures and textual references. Primary among
these were the adversary who tempts both Job in the Old
Testament and Christ in the New Testament, the rebel
leader of the fallen angels who became known as Lucifer
and was associated with the morning star, and the
serpent who tricked Eve in the Garden of Eden. Also
evident was the influence of the dualist ideology of the
Persian Zoroastrian religion, and the Devil's physical
appearance owes its origins to the old gods of pagan
Europe.

The Adversary

The Hebrew word *satan* means 'adversary', 'accuser' or
'obstructer'. In the Old Testament it seems to refer both
to angels and to humans and simply to denote one who
opposes or obstructs. In Numbers 22, for example, an
angel of the Lord places himself in the way of Balaam to
prevent him leaving: 'And God's anger was kindled
because he went: and the angel of the Lord stood in the
way for an adversary against him'. This is also the Islamic
understanding of Satan, and the equivalent Arabic word
is 'shaitan'.

In the Book of Job, an angel of the Lord with the title
of Satan, or Ha-Satan (the prefix 'Ha' simply meaning

'The'), takes on a more distinct and individuated personality but he is still a member of God's divine court. He acts only with the full permission of God and appears in Heaven before the throne of God, alongside the other 'Sons of God'. God asks Ha-Satan for his opinion regarding a man named Job, whom God considers to be 'perfect and upright'. Satan suggests that Job is only faithful because God showers him with riches and good fortune and asks for God's leave to test the faith of Job, attempting to provoke Job into cursing God by subjecting him to great adversity. His role here is not to *create* evil but rather to expose evil in the hearts of men by challenging their loyalty to God. Satan and God talk together with great familiarity and it seems clear that God has entrusted Satan to act on His behalf to uncover sinfulness.

In the New Testament Satan again appears as a more distinct personality, and this time he tests the faith of Christ Himself by tempting Him in the wilderness. We are not told if God has specifically sent Satan to perform this task, but he does appear to be reprising the role he took in the Book of Job.

The Fallen Angel
One persistent myth relating to the Devil is that he was once an angel in heaven, the highest of all the angels, but that he rebelled against God and was cast out of heaven and fell to earth. Various versions of the story blame the angel's fall on his pride and his refusal to bow down to God's creation, Adam. This version of the story appears in the Koran, where the angel is called Iblis. After his fall Iblis declares himself to be the enemy of mankind and

dedicates himself to leading them astray, starting with Adam and Eve (or 'Hawwa', as she is known in the Koran) in the Garden of Eden, whom he tricks into eating the forbidden fruit. In the Yezidi faith the angel is called Melek Ta'us (meaning 'God's Angel'), the Peacock Angel, who was the first created of all beings. According to Yezidi tradition, Melek Ta'us cried for 7,000 years in repentance for his disobedience and God forgave him. Melek Ta'us is the central deity of the Yezidi faith whose followers believe God gave the earth to be ruled over by him and that he is the Lord of This World.

Another version of the story tells how a group of angels descended to earth and intermarried with mortal women. The legend is only indirectly referred to in the Bible. Genesis 6 briefly alludes to the story:

And it came to pass, when men began to multiply on the face of the earth, and daughters were born unto them. That the sons of God saw the daughters of men that they were fair; and they took them wives all of which they chose ... There were giants in the earth in those days; and also after that, when the sons of God came in unto the daughters of men, and they bare children to them, the same became mighty men which were of old, men of renown.

In the original Hebrew the word 'giants' was rendered as 'nephilim', meaning 'fallen ones', a word derived from 'naphal', meaning 'to fall'. The apocryphal First Book of Enoch further elaborates on this story. It tells how a group of about two hundred angels called the Grigori, or 'Watchers', was set by God to watch over humanity.

However, these Watchers, persuaded by their leaders Samyaza and Azazel, defied God and intermarried with mortal women, begetting children by them. The Grigori further angered God by teaching their mortal wives and children many previously secret angelic arts, including enchantments, metalwork, astrology, meteorology and the use of cosmetics. The children of this union were a race of giant demons called the Nephilim, who wrought havoc upon the earth, prompting God to send the Great Flood to wipe them out. God punished the Watchers by imprisoning them 'in the valleys of the earth' until Judgement Day.

The Morning Star

As the third brightest object in the sky after the sun and moon, the planet Venus, the morning star, has a long mythic association with the rebel leader of the fallen angels. In St Jerome's fifth-century Vulgate Latin translation of the Bible he uses the name Lucifer in a passage in Isaiah 14, which Jewish scholars generally agree refers to the oppressive Babylonian king Nebuchadnezzar:

> How art thou fallen from heaven, O Lucifer, son of the morning! how art thou cut down to the ground . . . For thou hast said in thine heart, I will ascend into heaven, I will exalt my throne above the stars of God . . . I will ascend above the heights of the clouds; I will be like the most high. Yet thou shalt be brought down to hell, to the sides of the pit.

In the original Hebrew this reference to Lucifer is given as 'Helel, Son of Shahar'. Helel was a Babylonian god of the morning star, whose father, Shahar, was god of the dawn. In his translation St Jerome uses the Roman name for the morning star, Lucifer, which means 'light bringer' or 'light bearer', the herald of dawn. Some Jewish scholars have suggested that, in comparing Nebuchadnezzar with the morning star, the Old Testament prophet was drawing on an older (probably Babylonian) myth concerning the morning star and its fall from heaven. Post-exile Jewish legend sees Samyaza suspended, like the morning star, between heaven and earth after being cast out of heaven, an idea echoed in the Second Book of Enoch, where Samyaza is called Sataniel, and which includes the passage, 'And I threw him out from the height with his angels, and he was flying in the air continuously above the bottomless.'

Whilst some modern Christians now believe that the name Lucifer should not be identified with Satan, the early Church Fathers believed that Lucifer, although not the proper name of the Devil, was the name that represented him in his fallen state.

The Problem of Evil

God, for the strictly monotheistic early Jews, was the sole author of creation, both good and evil, and they had no concept of a separate principle of evil. Isaiah 45:7 states: 'I form the light, and create darkness: I make peace, and create evil: I the Lord do all these things'. The exile of the Jews in Babylonia, however, was to have a profound and lasting effect on Jewish perceptions of the nature of evil. The Zoroastrian religion of their new Persian rulers was dualistic; the God of Light, Ahura Mazda, in his manifestation as the Spirit of Truth, was locked into a ceaseless battle with Ahriman, the Spirit of Falsehood. This battle between good and evil would rage until the end of time, when Ahura Mazda would ultimately triumph and Ahriman would finally be destroyed. In later post-exile Jewish thought Satan began to take on a distinct identity and personality of his own. Influenced by the figure of Ahriman, Satan became a repository of evil and a subversive agent, tempting mankind to turn away from God's goodness.

The influence of Persian dualism was inherent in Christianity from the start. For Christian theologians, God was unequivocally good. But the goodness of God left the early Church Fathers with a doctrinal problem. How could a benevolent and omnipotent God allow suffering and evil to exist in the world? Increasingly, the answer came in the form of a separate principle of evil, personified in the form of the Devil. The New Testament Satan was viewed as the adversary not just of mankind but of Christ as well, and thus the foundations were laid for the cosmic battle between the Kingdom of Christ and the Kingdom of Satan, who would, like Ahriman, finally be defeated at the Second Coming.

The Devil in the Middle Ages

The influence of Persian dualism became most pronounced in the ideas of medieval heretics such as the Bogomils and Cathars, many of whom practised extreme asceticism and greatly exaggerated the powers of Satan in the world. The Bogomils held that Satan was Christ's elder brother. According to many heretics, the world belonged entirely to Satan and he ruled over it like a prince or a god. They abhorred the flesh of their earthly incarnations and stressed the spiritual freedom of the Kingdom of Christ in the hereafter. Like Judaism before it, official Church doctrine never assigned Satan the same independence as the Persian Ahriman and, although he eventually assumed many of God's darker aspects as the creator of evil, Satan still acted only with the permission of the one true God. This theological distinction, however, had little impact on the masses and popular fears about the immanence of Satan's Kingdom and his ability to do evil were heavily swayed by heretical dualist thought, which elevated Satan to a position that was coeval with God.

The medieval scholastics ascribed certain powers to the Devil, and their view became the orthodox one, but they came nowhere near attributing to the Devil the same earthly power or position the heretics claimed he had. According to the scholastics, the Devil could not alter or create physical substance in any way, since this was the exclusive preserve of God as the sole creator of the universe. The Devil was restricted to working with God's creation and only with God's permission. The Devil was believed to inhabit the realm of air and, as a result, the scholastics believed that he and his demons had the ability to produce illusions and control local motion. They could take on physical appearance by compressing various vapours into aerial bodies. In this form, they could participate in certain acts, including sexual intercourse, and one highly controversial theory posited that, in this form, they could procreate with the use of borrowed semen. Alternatively the Devil and his demons could also possess the body of another and take control of that person's bodily functions. The Devil's power to produce illusions meant that he could delude people into believing they had been the subject of certain supernatural experiences when, in fact, they had only imagined them. When witches believed they flew or people complained that they had been magically transformed into animals, for example, the orthodox view insisted that they were merely suffering under delusions caused by the Devil.

Depictions of the Devil

When the gods of the old pagan religions became the Devil of the new they also gave Satan a new visual identity; his characteristic horns, tail and cloven hooves were borrowed directly from deities such as the Gaulish hunting god Cernunnos and the Greek nature god Pan. Popular names for the Devil like Old Nick, Old Horny, Old Scratch or Good Fellow were also taken straight from the Devil's pagan predecessors, who lingered on in popular folkloric beliefs throughout Europe long after the introduction of Christianity. The physical descriptions of the Devil that emerge during the Middle Ages and dominate witchcraft trials have very little in common with the Biblical Satan, and largely owe their characteristics to the old European pagan gods and animistic nature spirits who were demonised by the Christian clerics. As well as his classic Pan-like incarnation the Devil was also variously described as being a black man, a large black dog, a cat, a toad, a goat or other horned animal.

The origin of the Devil's appearance as a black man is unclear and first occurs in the eleventh century. Often he was simply described as a man *dressed* in black. A seventeenth century English witch named Jane Wallis typically described the appearance of just such a figure:

> ... there appeared in the shape of a man in black cloaths and blackish cloaths about five weeks past, and bid her good-morrow, and shee asked what his name was, and he said his name was Blackeman.

The many depictions of the Virgin Mary as black demonstrate that the colour black was not exclusively associated with the Devil, and descriptions of the Devil's black *clothing* may owe more to Northern European folkloric beliefs about the attire of the Faeries than to any specific religious or racial ideas. The perceived threat, both ideologically and militarily, posed by Islam in the Middle Ages is likely to have had at least some influence on the association of the Devil with the colour black and with descriptions of his black countenance. The Islamic scholar Idries Shah has noted that in Arabic the words *black*, *wise*, *knowledge* and *understanding* all come from the root sound FHM and that, among the Sufis, black is synonymous with wisdom. The word *sayed*, meaning 'prince', comes from the root sound SWD, which also means black. Shah also notes that the banner of the Prophet Mohammed was originally black and that the Kaaba, the Holy of Holies at Mecca, is draped in black. In medieval Europe, Islam was a very real enemy. The Arab occupation of Moorish Spain from the eighth to the fifteenth centuries brought Europe directly into contact with Islamic culture, and Islam became firmly identified with the Kingdom of Satan. The eleventh century, in which the Devil as black man makes his first recorded appearance, saw not only sustained military campaigns against the Moors in southern Spain but also the first Crusade to reclaim the Holy Land from the Muslim 'infidels' in 1095.

The great crusading order of the Knights Templar was itself suppressed for heresy between 1307 and 1314 and was accused of having completely relinquished control of the order to the Devil, whom the Templars were alleged to worship in the form of a black cat. The Templars were also charged with worshipping a false idol called *Baphomet*, in the form of a disembodied head. It has often been suggested that the name *Baphomet* derived from a misinterpretation of the name *Mahomet*, a variation of *Mohammed*, because the medieval Church erroneously believed that Muslims worshipped idols. However, a more likely derivation of the name seems to be from the Arabic word *abufihamat*. Many of the Templars would have been fluent in Arabic. According to Shah, *abufihamat* means 'father of understanding', and is closely related to the Sufi concept of the 'head of knowledge', representing the refinement of human consciousness – what Shah calls 'the symbol of the completed man'. Hugh de Payens, one of the founders of the Templars, was said to have displayed an image of three black human heads on his shield, and Shah identifies the black head, the Negro head and the Turk's or Saracen's head, still found in heraldry and old English pub names as a direct descendant of the Sufi heads of knowledge.

Debate still rages over whether the Templars were actually guilty of any of the charges levelled against them, which also included homosexuality, infanticide and invoking demons, or whether the charges were entirely politically motivated. However, the discovery in 1945 of a painting of a disembodied head that has been carbon-dated to around 1280 certainly throws an interesting new light on the Baphomet charges. The head, known as the 'Panel Painting', was uncovered in an outhouse in the small Somerset village of Templecombe, where it appears to have remained hidden for centuries. From 1185 onwards, Templecombe became the West of England base for the Templars' vast operations across Europe and the Middle East. The head now hangs in the village church, where it is more popularly believed to be the head of Christ as depicted on the Shroud of Turin or the Mandylion, although some have suggested it may in fact be the head of St John the Baptist.

The Devil was also often popularly depicted as the Goat of Mendes, an ancient Egyptian he-goat deity who was reputed to have copulated with his female followers in much the same way that the Devil was believed to copulate with his worshippers. Witches were sometimes depicted paying homage to Satan by kissing the anus of a goat, or goat-like figure. This kiss became known as the *Osculum Infame*, or Obscene Kiss, and both heretics and, later, witches were routinely accused of bestowing it on the Devil, in whatever form he appeared to them. The nineteenth-century occultist Eliphas Lévi took aspects of the Goat of Mendes and added them to his depiction of Baphomet, which he believed represented the balancing unity of the universe. Lévi depicted his Baphomet as a winged figure that was half-human, half-goat, with female breasts and a flaming torch sprouting from between his horns. Although this figure has now entered the popular imagination as the archetypal depiction of Satan, this was never Lévi's intention and Baphomet has very little to do with the Devil of the witchcraft trials, except in Lévi's own assertion that it was, in fact, Baphomet and not the Devil whom the witches really worshipped.

The Protestant Reformers

Satan's presence in the world was further strengthened and reinforced during the Reformation. The Reformation and Counter-Reformation movements both stressed the need for a personal militancy against the all-pervasive Kingdom of Satan, and the zeal of the new Protestant preachers was equally matched by the fervour of the Counter-Reformation Catholic reformers. Although the great witch-hunting age of the sixteenth and seventeenth centuries coincided with the Reformation and Counter-Reformation era, the Reformation itself cannot be seen as directly responsible for the sharp increase in the outbreaks of prosecutions for witchcraft that took place during the period. However, both reform movements played an indirect role in contributing to the rise in witch-hunting by focusing on Satan's diabolical power over the world.

Crucially, the great Protestant reformers like Martin Luther and Jean Calvin did not challenge or reject the accepted thinking about the Devil, and neither Luther nor Calvin deviated from the traditional Catholic view that, although the Devil's power was great, he still needed the permission of God to act and would inevitably be defeated at the end of the world. However, both thinkers heavily emphasised the awesome nature of Satan's power and encouraged a climate of fear. Luther painted a very clear picture of the threat:

> Moreover, it cannot be denied but that the devil liveth, yea, and reigneth throughout the whole world ... Furthermore, we are all subject to the devil, both in body and goods; and we be strangers in this world, whereof he is the prince and god. Therefore the bread which we eat, the drink which we drink, the garments which we wear, yea, the air, and whatsoever we live by in the flesh, is under his dominion.

In many respects this statement closely resembles the dualist beliefs of the medieval Bogomil and Cathar heretics in declaring that the Devil was not only omnipresent and powerful in the world but that he was the natural ruler of it, the Prince of This World mentioned in John 12:31. Although he could not possibly defeat God, the Devil had the upper hand in this world, and Luther therefore enjoined every true Christian to be vigilant against the treacherous forces that were continually at work.

The writings of Jean Calvin clarified the scriptural foundations upon which this Protestant view of Satan's power rested. He emphasised the Devil's boldness and military-style prowess and insisted that he was an enemy in possession 'of every conceivable weapon and of skill in the science of warfare'. Calvin exhorted the true Christian to engage in military service and declare a lifetime of war on the Kingdom of Satan. 'If we are minded to affirm Christ's Kingdom as we ought,' he wrote, 'we must wage irreconcilable war with him who is plotting its ruin.'

2

THE PACT

Central to the development of the classic witchcraft stereotype was the belief that witches made a pact with the Devil in order to gain their supernatural powers and abilities. The development of this concept of the pact was instrumental in repositioning witchcraft as heresy and transforming the practitioners of simple *maleficia* and common sorcery into dangerous heretics who had renounced Christ in order to serve their new master, the Devil.

The Aristotelian worldview of the medieval scholastics convinced them that all forms of sorcery and magic lay in the realm of the Devil, and were at his command. God gave him permission to retain this power, but anything of a magical nature derived its efficacy from the Devil. According to this view there could be no such thing as 'white' or beneficent magic, and the scholastics argued that *anyone* who practised magic of any kind was dealing with the Devil. And the Devil, not known for his spontaneous generosity of spirit, didn't do anything without wanting something in return. Herein lay the seeds of the pact, as scholastic theologians began to surmise that, in order to carry out any kind of magical act, one would first have to offer the Devil some kind of recompense or reverence, and this amounted to nothing less than heresy and apostasy. The practitioner of magic was, by implication, denying God his supreme position in the universe and was offering to the Devil that which was due exclusively to God. St Thomas Aquinas, champion of Aristotle and the leading scholastic theologian of the thirteenth century, concerned himself with this question:

> It remains for us to inquire whence the magic arts derive their efficacy: a question that will present no difficulty if we consider their mode of operation . . . the significative words employed by the magician are *invocations*, *supplications*, *adjurations*, or even *commands* as though he were addressing another . . . Therefore the magic arts derive their efficacy from another intelligent being, to whom the magician's words are addressed . . . This is also proved by the sacrifices, prostrations and other similar practices, which can be nothing else than signs of reverence shown to an intellectual nature.

Demons and Demonologists

An important component in the medieval concept of magic was the knowledge and study of demons, which came to be known as *demonology*. Instrumental in inspiring the foundations of this demonology were the ideas about Lucifer and the fallen angels. Elaborate hierarchies of demons began to evolve amongst the demonologists who set about the task of categorising them and delimiting their individual powers. They had quite a list from which to choose. Estimates of the numbers of demons controlled by Satan often ran into the millions. Revelations 20:8 makes a reference to Satan's armies, 'the number of whom is as of the sand of the sea'.

The practice of a form of high magic known as *necromancy* became increasingly popular during the thirteenth century when many learned men began to conjure these demons in an attempt to gain hidden knowledge and perform acts of magic. Necromancy was practised in many royal and, perhaps rather surprisingly, even some Papal courts, and was the preserve of wealthy and well-educated men. Various *grimoires*, or books of magical instruction, began to appear describing the complex rituals necessary to conjure and control these demons. One of the most famous of these *grimoires* was the *Goetia, or Lesser Key of Solomon*, which gives details pertaining to seventy-two of the fallen angels. The *Goetia* tells the story of how King Solomon captured the fallen angels and locked them safely away in a container that was fastened with a magical seal. The container was later discovered, however, and the demons accidentally released, and the *grimoire* goes on to explain how the necromancer might command these demons and make them do his bidding by utilising certain aspects of the formula of Solomon's seal.

The learned necromancers, in their conjuration of demons, reinforced the beliefs of theologians that *all* acts of magic were performed with the aid of demons and thus the charge of heresy and pact began to attach itself to the low magic, or *maleficia*, of common witches as well. In 1398, after debating the matter, the scholastics at the University of Paris declared that *maleficia* was indeed a heresy. The theoretical difference that emerged between the learned necromancer and the common witch, however, amounted to the fine line between commanding a demon and serving one. The necromancer conjured demons in order to command them to perform acts of magic. He controlled the demons and compelled them to do his bidding. The lowly witch, on the other hand, was not considered nearly so clever and was merely the servant of the Devil, there to do *his* bidding in return for the power to commit magical acts. In terms of who was condemned for witchcraft and who wasn't this was an important distinction. The witch was guilty of explicit idolatry; the necromancer's actions only implied it.

Renaissance and Reformation Attitudes

Ever mindful of ending up on the wrong side of the torture chamber door the learned magicians, or *magi*, of the Renaissance sought to foster a clear distinction between their art and the art of the damnable witch, which they argued was little more than peasant superstition. They began to draw upon a sophisticated Neo-Platonic vision of the universe that moved the magic arts into the realm of natural science and away from any implications of demonic pact. Aristotelian scholasticism held a strictly rational and narrowly defined worldview; anything of an irrational nature was deemed to be outside the realm of the natural world and therefore supernatural and necessarily demonic in origin. The Neo-Platonism of the occult philosophers of the Renaissance widened the scope of what was considered natural. Renaissance Man and his universe were mutually and intrinsically connected by a 'world soul'. What happened on the microcosmic level had a corresponding effect on the macrocosmic level, and vice versa. According to the principle of 'as above, so below', it was now considered entirely natural, for example, that, as the planets traversed the skies above, the effects of their movements should be felt on the earth below and in the lives of men. Everything had a natural order and a corresponding effect, and was therefore measurable and predictable. Most importantly, all this occurred without any intervention from demons. It was the beginnings of a mechanistic view of the universe but it was a view that still had a soul. The highly influential *magus* Henry Cornelius Agrippa exemplified this approach and, in his 1531 text *De Occulta Philosophia* (translated into English as *Three Books of Occult Philosophy*), he described magic as 'this most perfect, and chief science, that sacred, and sublimer kind of philosophy, and lastly the most absolute perfection of all most excellent philosophy'.

The humanist arguments of the Renaissance *magi*, however, had no discernible impact on beliefs about or prosecutions for witchcraft, and it was not until the advent of Cartesian rationalism in the seventeenth century that a serious ideological challenge to the dominance of medieval scholasticism was finally mounted. The position of Renaissance sceptics like Agrippa and the German doctor Johann Weyer, who argued that those who believed themselves to be witches were actually suffering from a form of mental illness, proved largely ineffectual in changing the tide of opinion and belief. There were two major stumbling blocks to the position held by the Renaissance *magi*. Firstly, they failed to deny the existence of the Devil, to whom they still attributed the power to induce delusions and, secondly, they also failed to deny the efficacy of magic, which they still continued to practise, albeit with a Neo-Platonic flavour. As a result, the witch-hunting opposition found it easy to demolish their arguments against the reality of witchcraft, central to which were both the belief in the power of the Devil and in the efficacy of the witches' magic.

Reformation thought also reinforced the view that witches made pacts with the Devil and worshipped him as a false idol. Luther believed witches were not as common in his day as they had been when he was a child because the light of the revealed gospel had forced the Devil into retreat. But he still believed that witches made a covenant with the Devil and were therefore guilty of what he called 'spiritual sorcery', which was the be-witching of God. The bewitchment of God was, for Luther, a crime far more serious than merely bewitching cattle or children and he argued that witches were guilty of idolatry and should therefore be damned as heretics.

Cautionary tales about pacts with the Devil began to circulate throughout Europe as early as the ninth century. Archbishop Hincmar of Reims published a treatise in 860 warning against the dangers of magic in which he described one such pact. Desiring the atten-tions of a beautiful young girl, a boy approached a magician for help. The magician said he would gladly do what he could but that the boy must be prepared to renounce Christ in writing. The boy agreed and the magician set out a letter to the Devil, offering him the new recruit. The boy took the letter and that night held it up in the air and called out for the Devil. The Devil appeared and in a mockery of the Christian baptism asked the boy,

'Do you believe in me?'

'Yes,' replied the boy, 'I believe in you.'

'Do you renounce Christ?' the Devil went on.

'Yes,' responded the boy, 'I renounce Christ.'

The Devil then continued by telling the boy that he was fed up with Christians regularly coming to him and asking for his help and then relying on the mercy of Christ afterwards for forgiveness.

'I want you to sign up in writing,' he told the boy, 'so that you won't be able to back out later.'

The boy agreed, signed on the dotted line, and the Devil, as requested, caused the girl to fall in love with him. But, when the girl's father refused to let her marry the boy, the girl began to realise that she was in the Devil's power and, unable to stop loving the boy, she feared that she would die. Racked with guilt, the boy finally confessed and only with the intervention of St Basil was the girl released from her torments.

The Devils of Loudun

The trial of Father Urbain Grandier at Loudun in 1634 is one of the most famous trials in the history of European witchcraft and is, perhaps, one of the most notorious cases of an alleged pact with the Devil ever

recorded. In fact, so concrete was this pact that it was
actually produced as evidence in court, and the sheer
audacity and transparency of his politically inspired
persecutors cost Grandier his life in the most hideous
and cruel manner imaginable.

Father Urbain Grandier was the parish priest of St
Pierre du Marché in the town of Loudun in France.
Handsome, rich and charming, he wrote a treatise against
celibacy in the priesthood and liberally practised what he
preached amongst the local female population. He was
even rumoured to have fathered a child by Philippa
Trincant, the daughter of the king's solicitor. He was also
an opponent of Cardinal Richelieu, and was alleged to
have once penned a defamatory pamphlet against him. At
the time of the allegations against Grandier, Richelieu
was attempting to have Loudun's defensive battlements
demolished in his efforts to stamp out the Huguenots.
Both the Catholic and Protestant residents of Loudun
opposed Richelieu's intentions, fearing they would be
left defenceless against invading armies, and Grandier
managed to prevent the work from proceeding for a time.

The allegations against Grandier began when the
Mother Superior of the local Ursuline convent, Jeanne
des Anges, began to exhibit bizarre symptoms, falling
into convulsive fits and reporting sexually explicit
dreams in which Father Grandier tempted her to commit
lewd acts. It was not long before the other nuns began to
join in, as one contemporary witness observed:

> They struck their chests and backs with their heads, as if
> their necks were broken, and with inconceivable rapid-
> ity. They twisted their arms at the joints of the shoulder,

the elbow, or the wrist, two or three times around. Lying on their stomachs, they joined the palms of their hands to the soles of their feet; their faces became so frightful one could not bear to look at them; their eyes remained open without winking. Their tongues issued suddenly from their mouths, horribly swollen, black, hard, and covered with pimples . . . They threw themselves back till their heads touched their feet, and walked in this position . . . They uttered cries so horrible and so loud that nothing like it was ever heard before. They made use of expressions so indecent as to shame the most debauched of men, while their acts, both in exposing themselves and inviting lewd behaviour from those present would have astonished the inmates of the lowest brothels in the country.

Jeanne des Anges turned for help to Father Mignon, a relative of Philippa Trincant and an enemy of Grandier. Mignon, it is said, now saw the perfect opportunity to turn events in his favour and bring about Grandier's downfall. Some accounts suggest that it was Mignon who approached Jeanne des Anges and asked her to feign her symptoms in the first place. As Mignon set about exorcising the nuns, Jeanne des Anges announced that she was being possessed by two demons, Asmodeus and Zabulon, and that they had been sent to torment her by Father Grandier in the form of a bouquet of roses cast over the convent walls. Grandier, quite sensibly, became alarmed at the accusations against him and ordered that the nuns be confined to their cells. This failed and Grandier was forced to appeal to Archbishop Soudis of Bordeaux, who despatched his physician to examine the nuns. Finding no evidence of diabolical activity, Soudis ordered an end to the exorcisms and had the nuns confined to their cells. Peace was restored to the convent, but only for a few short months.

A priest named Jean de Laubardemont, a relative of Jeanne des Anges, had been sent to Loudun to carry out Cardinal Richelieu's orders to demolish the battlements. Thwarted in his efforts by Father Grandier, de Laubardemont reported the nuns' accusations to his boss. Richelieu, who also had a relative in the convent, wasted no time in forming a committee to investigate the matter and to perform public exorcisms on the nuns. Among the crack team of exorcists sent to work on the nuns, which included the Capuchin Father Tranquille and the Franciscan Father Lactane, was a Jesuit named Jean-Joseph Surin. The exorcisms were to have tragic consequences for Father Surin, who was eventually driven mad by the experience and tried to commit suicide some years later. In a letter to a friend and fellow Jesuit, written in May 1635, Surin described in vivid detail how he too had become convinced that he was possessed by demons:

> There is not just one demon who works on me, but two ordinarily; one of them is Leviathan, the opposite of the Holy Ghost, in as much as they have said here that they have a Trinity in Hell that the Witches worship, Lucifer, Beelzebub, and Leviathan, who is the third Person of Hell, and several authors have remarked and written on this heretofore. Now, the actions of this false Paraclete are completely the opposite of the true one, and they impart a desolation that one could never describe adequately. He is the leader of the entire group of our Demons, and he is the supervisor of the whole affair, which is the strangest that perhaps has ever been seen.

The exorcisms became a public spectacle and sometimes as many as 7,000 people were in attendance. The outrage against Grandier grew and a string of former mistresses came forward to accuse him of depravity and sacrilegious acts, reinforcing the belief that Grandier was truly diabolical in nature. In November 1633, Grandier was arrested and imprisoned in the Castle of Angers. A surgeon named Mannouri, another of Grandier's enemies, was summoned and he soon discovered a Devil's Mark.

At Grandier's trial evidence against him was produced in the form of a written pact, which had apparently been stolen from Lucifer's personal collection by the demon Asmodeus. The document had been written in Latin from right to left and was allegedly signed in blood by Grandier and witnessed by a selection of demons, one of whom, seemingly illiterate, had signed his name with a drawing of a pitchfork. Disturbed by the way the trial was proceeding, some of the nuns attempted to retract their accusations against Grandier. Jeanne des Anges even appeared in court with a rope around her neck and threatened to hang herself, claiming that she had perjured herself and wanted to recant. The nuns' efforts were dismissed by the court as a ploy by Satan to save one of his own. Witnesses were threatened with arrest if they testified in favour of Grandier and some were even forced to flee the country. On 18 August 1634, Grandier was convicted:

> . . . we have condemned and shall condemn this Grandier to make honourable repentance, bare-headed, a rope around his neck, bearing in his hand a burning torch

weighing two pounds, before the main door of the Church of St Pierre du Marché, and before that of St Ursula of this said town, and there, upon his knees, to ask pardon of God, of the King and of Justice; and this accomplished, to be taken to the public square of Sainte Croix, to be attached to a stake upon a pyre, which will be constructed at the said square for this purpose, and there to be burned alive with the pacts and the signs of Sorcery lying on the pyre, together with his Manuscript Book against priestly celibacy, and his ashes scattered to the wind ...

Grandier was subjected to hideous and excruciating torture, administered by Father Tranquille. His legs were crushed to a pulp in a contraption known as the Boots but he steadfastly refused to confess or to name accomplices. He was dragged to the public square and burned alive, without the mercy of first being garrotted. His death, however, did not put an end to the antics of the nuns, and it was not until Cardinal Richelieu eventually acted to cut off their funds several years later that the whole chapter was finally brought to a close.

The Familiar Spirit
Closely allied with the idea of the pact was the concept of the familiar. The notion that witches had pet demons that they named and cared for became popular in the fourteenth century, particularly in England and Germany. The quirky and often humorous names attributed to these familiars, such as Sacke and Sugar, Vinegar Tom, or Pecke in the Crown, testify to their origins as pagan nature spirits, Faeries and imps, which had been gradual-

ly demonised under Christianity. Necromancers had long been thought to conjure demons but it was not until the late thirteenth century that these folk spirits began to be firmly associated with witchcraft. The idea of pact was inherent in the witches' dealings with their familiars and they were regularly accused of having suckled the demons with their own blood in return for magical assistance. The accused were often searched for evidence of a 'witch's teat', which they were believed to use for this purpose.

Witches' familiars usually took the form of a small animal such as a cat, although sometimes they were thought to exist in non-material form. The association between demons and animals was an old one, and it had long been believed that both demons and sorcerers could transform themselves at will into the shapes of animals. So strong was the association between the pact and the animal familiar at the trial of Elizabeth Francis at Chelmsford in 1566 that, without due formality, her prosecutors got straight to the point and accused her of possessing a cat who was actually called Satan. Her grandmother was said to have 'counselled her to renounce God and his word and to give of her blood to Satan... which she delivered her in the likeness of a white spotted cat'. Demonstrating his metamorphic prowess, the satanic cat was also alleged to have transformed himself into both a toad and a black dog during the course of events.

3

THE SABBAT

As important as the Pact was the idea that witches met in organised groups to worship the Devil collectively. Belief in the reality of these Sabbats played a crucial role in the whole witch-hunting mechanism. Without the conviction that witches met together in concert the trials of individual witches would not have involved the search for accomplices and the characteristic chain-reaction witch-hunts that typified the Witch Craze would not have developed in the manner that they did.

The idea of the Sabbat did not become fully established until the fifteenth century and even then was sometimes paid scant regard. The infamous witch-hunting manual *Malleus Maleficarum*, published in 1486, barely mentions the Sabbat, making only slight reference to 'a congress of women in the night-time' and 'a ceremony . . . when witches meet together in conclave on a set day'. The key features of the classic Sabbat are that it occurred at night and in secret; the witches gathered to pay homage to the Devil, renounce Christ and make pacts; and that feasting and obscene, anti-human behaviour took place. This behaviour usually involved infanticide and cannibalism, indiscriminate orgies and other perverse sexual activity, including the Obscene Kiss. In some descriptions, usually those of France, Italy and Spain, parodies of the Catholic mass also appear, the sacrament or cross is sometimes desecrated and prayers are said backwards. However, the infamous Black Mass was never a part of classic witchcraft and seems rather to have originated amongst the licentious aristocracy of late seventeenth-century Paris. Some witches confessed to attending the Sabbat every Thursday night, whilst others attended only once or twice a year, usually on the old pagan festivals of May Eve, often known as Walpurgisnacht (30 April), and Hallowe'en (31 October). The numbers of witches attending any one particular Sabbat could range wildly from a handful to many thousands, sometimes with entire villages being implicated.

Heretical Activity
The biggest influence on the formation of the Sabbat originated in allegations levelled against medieval heretics such as the Cathars and Waldensians, and these allegations can, in turn, be traced back to Roman beliefs about the early Christians. The word *Sabbat* seems to have been a derivative of *Sabbath*, and was probably a deliberate anti-Jewish slur. Both witches' and heretics' nocturnal assemblies were also sometimes referred to as *synagogues*. The word *coven* does not appear anywhere

in continental witchcraft and was first used by Isobel Gowdie in seventeenth-century Scotland.

The Romans accused the early Christians of regularly indulging in human sacrifice, cannibalism and incestuous orgies. The Communion was widely misunderstood to involve real human flesh and the blood of a sacrificed child. During the second-century Roman persecution of Christians at Lyon and Vienne, slaves were tortured until they confessed that their Christian masters were involved in ritual incest and cannibalism in which both adults and children were killed and eaten. Some early Christian fathers began to counter these lurid allegations by claiming that it was, in fact, the Jews and the Romans who really practised these things and, around AD 150, Justin Martyr was the first orthodox Christian openly to accuse Christian heretics of being responsible for such acts. The Marcionites, he said, did indeed practise cannibalism and incest and they were to blame for the terrible slur on Christianity. Justin Martyr was also the first to claim that these heretics held their incestuous orgies 'with the lights extinguished', a phrase which later became standard in descriptions of the witches' Sabbat.

Other Christian fathers began to follow suit and to accuse various heretical Christian sects of actually indulging in incestuous orgies and infanticide. Tertullian introduced the idea that not only were the lights extinguished at these heretical orgies but that they were done so in an unusual manner: dogs, he claimed, were tied to the lamps and, when it was time for the lights to be extinguished, the dogs would be tempted away with scraps of meat, thus overturning the lamps. Again, this detail found its way, almost word for word, into later descriptions of the Sabbat. The tone was now set for what became the standard denunciation of Christian heretics that was later liberally applied to medieval sects like the Cathars and Waldensians. The heretics held secret revels after dark, usually underground, where the lights were extinguished and each attendee grabbed the person nearest to them and indulged in indiscriminate copulation. They invoked demons, paid homage to the Devil with the Obscene Kiss, and children were stolen, killed and eaten, or food prepared from their blood. Sometimes embryos, semen and menstrual blood were also consumed in a perverse parody of the Communion.

These allegations resurfaced in the eleventh century at the trial at Orléans in 1022 of the alleged members of an heretical sect of high-ranking priests. The accused were burnt at the stake, a punishment of unusual severity for the time, and the charges seem to have been manufactured to further the political motives of King Robert II, who intervened to pronounce a death sentence when the churchmen trying the case began to express doubts about the validity of the charges. The trial is important in the history of witchcraft because, as well as regurgitating the (by now) familiar clerical clichés of nocturnal orgies, devil-worship, invocation of demons, blasphemy, cannibalism and child sacrifice that later became standard features in trials for witchcraft, it also introduces two new allegations that were to become central to the concept of witchcraft. Firstly, the heretics allegedly claimed that, when possessed by the Holy Spirit, they could be magically and instantaneously transported from one place to another, and secondly, they reportedly said that the Devil appeared to them in the form of a black man. This is the earliest known reference to the Devil as a black man, and the earliest association of magical flight with heretical activities. Despite its early date this trial is recognisably witch-like and, for the first time, it assembles in one place many of the main components of the later witches' Sabbat.

The First Heretic Witches

The first trial to link explicitly the charges of witchcraft and heresy was that of Lady Alice Kyteler, in Ireland in 1324. The concept of classic witchcraft had still not been completely formed at this early stage and, unlike the heretics at Orléans, Lady Alice and her accomplices did not face the more outrageous charges of cannibalism and infanticide. They were not alleged to have flown to their nocturnal meetings nor to have made a pact with the Devil. However, it is the first trial to portray witches as members of an organised sect of heretics who collectively worshipped the Devil. Lady Alice evaded arrest and escaped to England under the protection of her powerful friends before her trial could take place, and she was condemned in her absence. She was excommunicated and her wealth and possessions confiscated, although it is not known what became of them. Her maid, Petronilla de Meath, was not so lucky and became the first heretic, and the first witch, to be burnt at the stake in Ireland.

Relatively complete records of the case have survived and they tell a fascinating story of drama and political intrigue. Lady Alice was a wealthy Kilkenny noblewoman. She had outlived three husbands and her fourth, Sir John Power, lay seriously ill. Rumours reached Sir John via one of the maids that his wife was trying to poison him and, after seizing some powders and potions found amongst his wife's private belongings, which he claimed were evidence of witchcraft, he was not slow in reporting the matter to Bishop Richard Ledrede of Ossory. The stepchildren from Lady Alice's previous marriages supported the accusations and began to claim that she had bewitched their fathers to death as well and robbed them of their rightful inheritance.

Bishop Ledrede summoned Lady Alice, now living with her favourite son, the wealthy banker William Outlaw, to appear before him. However, the bishop's men, upon arriving at Outlaw's house to issue the summons, found that Lady Alice had escaped to Dublin, out of the bishop's jurisdiction. The bishop attempted to have her arrested but was denied authorisation from the king. Lady Alice and her supporters then turned the tables on Bishop Ledrede and he found himself arrested and jailed for seventeen days by the Seneschal of Kilkenny, who described him as a 'vile, interloping monk'. Eventually Bishop Ledrede took matters into his own hands and travelled to Dublin to file for a civil arrest. He was too late. Lady Alice had already fled to England with Petronilla de Meath's daughter Sarah.

The bishop now turned his attention to the citizens of Kilkenny, where he conducted three inquisitions. Lady Alice was condemned as a heretic and a sorcerer and charges were brought against eleven of her alleged accomplices, including her son William Outlaw and her maid Petronilla de Meath. Also accused were Petronilla's daughter Sarah (also known as Basilia), Robert of Bristol, Alice Faber, John Galrussyn, Helen Galrussyn, Syssoh Galrussyn, William Payne de Boly, Eva de Brounestoun and Annota Lange. A contemporary account known as the *Narrative*, believed to have been written by either Ledrede or one of his supporters, notes that 'only the poorer ladies' were then arrested and imprisoned by the Seneschal and his officers who had quite openly allowed Lady Alice herself to escape.

Lady Alice and her associates were accused of renouncing Christ and sacrificing to a demon called Robin, Son of Art, or Robin Artisson. They met at midnight at a lonely crossroads and offered sacrifices of nine red cocks and nine peacocks' eyes to Robin who was also alleged to be Lady Alice's demon lover, or incubus. Sometimes he appeared in the form of a cat, a black dog, or as an Ethiop (a common term used to denote a black man). On occasion two taller men, each of whom carried an iron rod, accompanied him. Petronilla de Meath allegedly confessed to seeing three black men, each carrying an iron rod, and that she had been present when Lady Alice and Robin Artisson had sexual intercourse. Lady Alice was also accused of having nightly swept the streets of Kilkenny with a broom, sweeping all the filth and muck to her son William's door and muttering, 'To the house of William my son, here lie all the wealth of Kilkenny town.' The accused were also said to have cast spells using ointments and powders made from dead men's fingernails and the shrouds of unbaptised babies, which they cooked up in a cauldron made from the skull of an executed criminal.

Petronilla de Meath was flogged six times on the orders of the bishop and on 3 November 1324 was condemned to death. She was burnt at the stake before a huge crowd of people, having utterly refused to repent or accept the Christian sacrament. The *Narrative* reports that the 'other heretics and soothsayers belonging to that pestiferous society of Robin Artisson were dealt with according to the law'. All except William Outlaw, whose considerable political connections allowed him to be released from prison after he agreed to recant his heresies publicly and to re-roof Kilkenny's cathedral with lead. The political fallout from Bishop Ledrede's relentless pursuit of Lady Alice and her associates was considerable. The bishop made some powerful enemies and it was Lady Alice who ultimately triumphed. Upon her escape to England she lived comfortably under the protection of King Edward III, who seized Ledrede's revenues in 1329. The Archbishop of Dublin accused Ledrede himself of heresy and he was forced into exile in disgrace.

A second notable trial to link heretical activity with witchcraft took place in Switzerland between 1397 and 1406. In some ways the trial is more important than that of Lady Alice because it took place not in an ecclesiastical court but in a secular one. Moreover, the charge was not one of heresy but of simple *maleficia*. The accused, a man named Stedelen, was charged with various acts of *maleficia*, including blasting crops and bewitching cattle. Under torture, he confessed to belonging to a sect of Devil worshippers who conjured demons, renounced Christ, and murdered babies to make magical ointments. Stedelen's trial demonstrates how, by the end of the fourteenth century, a legal transition was taking place. Magistrates were beginning to take the previously spiritual crime of heresy and merge it with the secular crime of *maleficia*.

Witches were often confused with heretics and a great deal of misunderstanding frequently arose over who was a witch and who was a standard heretic. The term *Waudenses* (from *Waldensian*) was indiscriminately applied to witches and the related word *vauderie* became a common term for the Sabbat. However, a number of witch trials in the Swiss and French Alps in the 1420s and 1430s suggest that the inquisitors did seem to believe they were dealing with a new and distinct sect, unconnected with the other heretics. Many of the standard charges involving the Sabbat were directly influenced by beliefs about heretics but heretics were only very rarely accused of two specific charges that are central to classic witchcraft, namely *maleficia* and flying to nocturnal gatherings. The alpine witches were accused of flying to Sabbats where they took part in orgies and feasted on the flesh of murdered babies. By the time of these trials it had been around three centuries since any heretic had actually been prosecuted for alleged infanticide or cannibalism, yet these charges were brought against the alpine witches at a time when many Waldensian heretics were also being prosecuted in the same locale, suggesting that these witches were not being confused with the heretics but were considered to be a separate sect.

At about the same period the wandering preacher Bernardino of Siena was travelling around Italy, condemning witches and telling stories of secret nocturnal gatherings where members of a diabolical witch cult murdered babies and drank potions made from the dust of their ground-up remains. In 1437, the Dominican monk Johannes Nider completed his influential work *Formicarius* (The Ant Heap) in which he alleged that practitioners of *maleficia* belonged to a secret sect that murdered babies, ate their flesh, and used the boiled remains to make potions to drink and other magical charms and ointments. In Ireland, Bishop Ledrede, ever ahead of his time it seems, had referred to a 'new and pestilential sect in our parts' as early as around 1320. As the threat posed by real heretics began to recede, this new sect of witches began to take on many of the anti-human characteristics originally associated with the heretics. A new organised conspiracy from within was starting to emerge that would gradually replace the old.

4

NIGHT FLIGHT

The idea that witches flew to their Sabbats had its roots in the pagan custom of the night ride, or wild hunt, and is one of the strongest indicators of the influence that the pagan goddess Diana and her localised counterparts had on the formation of the classic witchcraft stereotype. Also influential were the pagan legends of blood-sucking *strigae* or *lamiae*, owl-like demon women who were believed to fly through the air at night and suck the blood of humans. These beliefs were themselves largely influenced by the legends of the baby-killing demons Lilith and Lamia. Lilith, according to Hebrew legend, was the first wife of Adam, created not from his rib but from the earth, just as he was. This convinced Lilith that she was Adam's equal, not his inferior. After a good deal of marital strife she flew off and left him in order to live in the desert with her demon lovers. Lilith became a demonic and vengeful figure who took the life of newborn babies in return for the lives of her own demon children. Similarly the Libyan queen Lamia also became a baby-killer after the murder of her own children at the hands of the goddess Hera, who discovered that Lamia was the lover of her husband Zeus. The grief-stricken Lamia is then said to have taken her own revenge by killing the children of other people. These separate and distinct folk beliefs gradually became confused and, over the course of the later Middle Ages, the stereotype of the diabolical flying witch was born.

The belief that witches flew was not universally accepted and much debate took place about whether witches actually flew to their Sabbats or merely imagined that they flew. These two opposing ideas coexisted for some time and the idea that witches actually flew, although it eventually became the prevailing concept, never really found full acceptance. Flying, for instance, does not figure in cases of witchcraft in England, and English law never made magical flight an offence. Continental witches were popularly believed to fly to their Sabbats on the backs of demons in the shape of animals, on forked sticks, pitchforks and shovels, in baskets, or more frequently on broomsticks. Scotland's witches flew in sieves and on bean and straw stalks.

Flying Ointment
Another popular belief about witches was that they flew with the aid of a special ointment which was given to them when they first signed their pact with the Devil. Some believed that this ointment physically caused the witches to fly, whilst others believed that it led to the illusion of flying, or allowed the witch to fly and attend

the Sabbat 'in spirit', when in fact she was still asleep in her bed. This argument was popular as a defence against claims by the accused that they could not possibly have been at the Sabbat because they were asleep beside their husbands in bed at the time it was alleged to have taken place. Another argument to counter this particular claim was that the witches left demons in bed in their place when they flew off to the Sabbat, so their husbands would never know they were missing.

Various recipes for these so-called flying ointments have been recorded and recent scientific experiments have analysed some of them. These experiments show that a significant number of the recipes really did contain hallucinogenic ingredients that not only cause the sensation of flying but also make the user believe they have been travelling across vast expanses of terrain and undergoing strange erotic experiences. The somewhat theatrical recipes may call for gruesome ingredients such as the fat of unbaptised babies, soot and bat's blood but the active ingredients that probably produced the real effects were powerful and very dangerous herbs such as belladonna, henbane and aconite. Abraham the Jew reported an experience with a witch and her flying ointment in *The Book of the Sacred Magic of Abramelin the Mage*, published in 1458. Abraham encountered the witch in Linz in Austria, where she gave him some ointment to rub on his pulse points. After doing so, he then experienced the vivid sensation of flying through the air and arriving at the place he had wished to visit. After this initial experience Abraham decided upon a second experiment in which he asked the witch to use the ointment to visit a friend of his and, on her return, to describe what she had seen. She rubbed the ointment on her wrists and feet but, instead of flying away, as Abraham had expected, she fell to the floor as though dead and there she remained, inert, for some hours. When she finally came round she described the journey she had been on, but it did not correspond in any way to what the reality of a journey to his friend should have been. Abraham concluded that the ointment induced fantastical dream flights, not real ones.

The Night Ride

In many ways the belief that witches flew to their Sabbats was a necessary one if their persecutors were to argue, as they frequently did, that the witches' Sabbats took place in remote and inaccessible regions. New-foundland was one popular nocturnal destination for witches. Medieval scholasticism had established that the Devil, having power over local motion, could magically lift and transport people through the air and set them down great distances away. But on the whole the scholastics were fairly sceptical and, for the most part, concurred with the official doctrine of the Church, as laid out in the *Canon Episcopi*, where it was made clear that the belief in flying was an illusion induced by the Devil, and that it was therefore wrong to believe that witches flew out at night. The *Canon Episcopi* appeared around 1140, and warned bishops that they must 'labour with all their strength to uproot thoroughly from their parishes the pernicious art of sorcery and malefice invented by the Devil'. It then goes on to condemn the pagan custom of the Dianic procession:

... some wicked women, perverted by the Devil, and seduced by illusions and phantasms of demons, believe and profess themselves, in the hours of night, to ride upon certain beasts with Diana, the goddess of pagans, and an innumerable multitude of women, and in the silence and the dead of night to traverse great spaces of earth, and to obey her commands as of their mistress, and to be summoned to her service on certain nights.

According to the *Canon Episcopi* it was the *belief* that women rode out at night with Diana that was wrong, because this belief was nothing more than an illusion caused by the Devil. Belief in the night ride was a 'false opinion' and those who believed in it wandered 'from the right faith' and were 'involved in the error of the pagans when they think that there is anything of divinity or power except the one God'. It was this 'error' that was later to cause so much debate, as popular belief began to assign powers to the Devil that the *Canon Episcopi* assigned exclusively to God. Gradually argument grew over whether witches, with the aid of the Devil, could actually fly or not. By the end of the fifteenth century the Dominican authors of the witch-hunting manual *Malleus Maleficarum* had capitalised on the ambiguity of the *Canon Episcopi* and invented an ingenious get-out clause. The *Malleus* carefully implied that, although canon law stated that it was wrong for witches to believe they flew, it might not necessarily follow that they didn't actually fly anyway. After all, asks the *Malleus*, 'who is so foolish as to conclude that they cannot *also* be bodily transported?'

The night ride referred to by the *Canon Episcopi*, also known in certain parts of Europe as 'the wild hunt', was a lingering pagan belief which the Church was keen to stamp out. Many women were believed to join the spirits of the dead in nocturnal processions led by Diana, in which they rode on the backs of beasts, and went from house to house performing beneficent acts. In France and Italy these women were known as the Good Society, Women of the Good Game, or *Bonae.* In Germany the fertility goddess Holda, or Perchta, was the leader of this procession, where it was known as 'the wild hunt', 'wild chase' or 'wild ride'. Holda also led the Furious Horde, the spirits of those who had died young, across the skies at night.

In late fourteenth-century Milan two women were separately accused of attending the society of Signora Oriente, who seems to have been a localised version of Diana. The first of these two women, Sibillia, appeared before Milan's secular court in 1384, charged with heresy. It was alleged that she and the other members of her society went out every Thursday night to pay homage to Oriente, who taught them the art of divination. They feasted together and consumed every type of animal, except the ass, which, according to Sibillia, was sacred to Christ and therefore not on the menu. Sibillia refused to believe that she had committed any type of sin, but was found guilty and given a penance. Some years later Sibillia was found to have relapsed and was re-arrested. She admitted that she had been attending the society again, and that she had paid homage to Diana. She also admitted that she had been attending the games of Diana, as they were also known, since she was a child. This time she added that members dared not speak the name of God because it was very offensive to Signora Oriente.

The second case of a woman charged with attending the society of Signora Oriente was that of Pierina de Bugatis in 1390. Pierina claimed that Signora Oriente ruled over her society in the same way Christ ruled over the world. Every animal except the ass and the wolf attended the society, along with the spirits of the dead. The animals were eaten but were resurrected by Oriente immediately afterwards. Oriente taught her followers the secrets of magic and they went from house to house at night, stealing food from the houses of the rich and blessing the houses of the poor. The case was referred to the Inquisition and ecclesiastical ideas linking heresy with witchcraft immediately and very clearly began to creep in, transforming Pierina's activities from the vestiges of pagan belief and custom into a case of diabolical witchcraft. Now Pierina was alleged to have signed a pact with the Devil in her own blood and called upon a demon called Lucifel, who appeared to her in the form of a man and conveyed her through the air to the meetings of the society.

5

LEGAL REMEDIES

Although a profound fear of the Devil and a belief in the diabolical threat posed by his human recruits were necessary preconditions for the Witch Craze, the actual process of witch-hunting was essentially legal in nature and, without the correct legal foundations, the Witch Craze would have failed to ignite. As with so many other areas of medieval life, fundamental changes began to take place within Europe's legal systems during the period that would dramatically alter the way in which crime was dealt with and create the necessary framework for the effective prosecution of both heretics and witches.

Although many individual prosecutions for witchcraft occurred from the medieval period onward, the legal process against individual witches usually developed into an organised hunt for accomplices. These witch-hunts were largely characterised by their chain-reaction mechanism in which defendants were pressed, usually through the use of torture, to denounce and name fellow witches. These were themselves then subjected to the same process until an initial accusation of witchcraft had radiated outwards, often across an entire community. Sometimes the hunts remained small in scale, with only a handful of suspected witches being uncovered in this way, but, when left unchecked, the tally of accused sometimes ran into tens or hundreds and ultimately caused severe dysfunction of the affected communities as a result.

Changes in Criminal Procedure

Prior to the thirteenth century, the prosecution of crime was largely the responsibility of the private individual who would accuse the defendant at a public tribunal. If no proof or confession were forthcoming then innocence or guilt would be determined, not by a rational examination of the facts, but by an appeal to God to intervene and dispense justice. The process by which God's will was usually interpreted was known as the 'ordeal', in which the accused was required to undergo some kind of physical test. This test often took the form of carrying a hot iron or dipping an arm into boiling water. The injuries sustained by the accused were examined after a few days for signs of healing. It was believed that God would protect the innocent and cause their wounds to miraculously heal but, if the wounds had not healed, the defendant was found guilty. Other alternatives to the trial by ordeal were trial by combat, in which a duel was fought either directly by the two parties involved or indirectly by their champions, or trial by water, in which the accused was thrown into a pond or river and their innocence or guilt determined by whether they sank or floated. If a person was found to be innocent they were then entitled to bring a counter-suit against their original accuser, following the old Roman convention of *lex talionis*. This early medieval judicial system has become known as the 'accusatorial' system, and was essentially a non-rational system in which God was deemed to be the sole judge. Although a mortal judge presided over the proceedings, he was not in any way responsible for the prosecution of the accused or for determining the outcome of the case.

During the thirteenth century a new style of criminal prosecution, based on the revival of Roman law, began to replace the old accusatorial system throughout Western Europe. The new system has become known as 'inquisitorial' procedure and took the prosecution of crime out of the hands of the individual and placed it into the hands of the judicial authorities. This new, rationalised method focused on the systematic discovery of the facts by gathering all the available evidence. The judge and his officials interviewed witnesses, interrogated the accused, recorded their statements and reached a verdict based on the established facts of the case. Accusations by private individuals were still possible but the judicial authorities now assumed responsibility for the prosecution of cases and had the power to initiate prosecutions themselves, based on their own knowledge of the situation, even if this amounted to little more than rumour and hearsay.

At around the same time as this inquisitorial system was developing on the Continent, England was also beginning to abandon accusatorial procedure in favour of the jury system. Two types of jury developed in England, the *presenting jury*, which acted on behalf of the king to examine and review all public prosecutions, and the *trial jury*, which reached a verdict in each individual case. Initially, trial juries were active in establishing the facts of a case and it was not until the sixteenth century that the trial jury began to sit as a passive panel, considering the evidence presented to it by legal professionals. Scotland's legal system combined elements of both the English and continental systems, with judges actively gathering and compiling prosecution evidence, as on the Continent, but with a trial jury responsible for returning the verdict.

The Birth of the Inquisition

In its bid to stamp out heresy the Catholic Church became the driving force behind this new approach to investigating and prosecuting crime. The problem of heresy began increasingly to concern the Church in the late twelfth and early thirteenth centuries. In 1184 a papal bull was issued instructing bishops to identify heretics for prosecution by the secular courts. The Fourth Lateran Council in 1215 not only demanded the death penalty for unrepentant heretics but also forbade priests from taking part in the ordeal. As the ordeal required a priest's blessing before it could take place, the Council's decree was pivotal in pushing the secular authorities into abandoning accusatorial justice altogether and adopting the new inquisitorial procedures. A formal ecclesiastical body dedicated solely to seeking out and prosecuting heretics was created around 1227, in the shape of the Inquisition, and was staffed by the Dominican and Franciscan mendicant orders. In 1231, Pope Gregory IX issued the papal bull *Excommunicamus* in which the Inquisition's constitution was formally laid out. Initially, the Inquisition only operated in Germany but, in 1232, it moved into the Aragon region of Spain and, by the following year, it had expanded across Europe.

In the past, the role of the Catholic Church and the Inquisition in witch-hunting has been over-emphasised and they have been regularly blamed for almost entirely inventing and sustaining the crime of witchcraft. Recent work by historians on trial records has begun to show a somewhat different picture, however, and it is now estimated that both the Inquisition and other ecclesiastical courts were probably only responsible for less than 50% of the total number of prosecutions for witchcraft. The secular courts were to become the major force behind witch-hunting and the role of the ecclesiastical courts gradually declined. The Church had always relied heavily on the assistance of the secular courts in bringing heretics to justice and carrying out executions, which the Church did not have the power to do. By adapting and extending their traditional jurisdiction over *maleficia*, the secular courts gradually began to assume control over the 'spiritual' crime of witchcraft as well and, by the sixteenth century, most European states had incorporated specific laws against witchcraft into their legislature.

The Introduction of Torture
Because the new inquisitorial procedure now relied on human rather than divine judgement the requirements for proving guilt were necessarily more stringent. On the

Continent the old Roman laws against treason became the basis of the new inquisitorial standard known as the romano-canonical law of proof. This required either the testimonies of two eyewitnesses to the crime or a confession from the accused. English juries, by contrast, were able to return a guilty verdict based only on circumstantial evidence or on the testimony of one eyewitness. The problem with prosecuting heresy, and by extension witchcraft, was that it was, by its very nature, a concealed crime and therefore highly unlikely to result in any reliable eyewitnesses. Both heretics and witches were believed to commit their diabolical acts in total secrecy and heresy was, after all, essentially a crime of belief. This began to present a serious challenge to the judicial operation to suppress heresy, and led directly to the introduction of torture as a means of gaining confessions from the accused. The first recorded use of torture to obtain confessions from criminals was in the secular jurisdiction of Verona in 1228 and the Church followed suit in 1252, permitting inquisitors to use torture in cases of suspected heresy.

The reliability of confessions extracted under torture does not seem to have been considered problematic and there seems to have existed an overriding conviction that God would protect the innocent and allow them to withstand torture in much the same way as He had protected them against the ordeal. The use of torture was, in theory, regulated by strict rules governing its application but, in practice, these rules were routinely flouted or entirely disregarded, especially by the secular courts. The original rules concerning the use of torture left little room for misuse by over-zealous judges and, had they been properly adhered to, it is unlikely that witch-hunting would ever have evolved in the way that it did. The rules stipulated that a crime must first of all be proven to have occurred. Had this rule alone been enforced then any attempt at witch-hunting should theoretically have fallen at the first hurdle. The proof required was either one eyewitness testimony or some kind of circumstantial evidence that could be considered the legal equivalent of an eyewitness. If no other way of establishing the facts was available then torture was permitted but only after the defendant had first been threatened with its use. Once applied, the torture could not be reapplied and the defendant must repeat their confession freely outside the torture chamber for it to be legally admissible. In 1376, the papal inquisitor Nicholas Eymeric published a manual for inquisitors in which he conveniently sidestepped the restriction on reapplying torture by stating that it was quite acceptable for torture to be *continued* at a later date, thus opening the door for the eventual use of unlimited applications of torture.

Any form of torture was not theoretically allowed to draw blood, maim or kill. The most common forms of torture therefore involved distending the body or crushing the extremities. Tortures that were routinely applied included the *pinniewinks*, or thumbscrews, used to crush the fingers; *thrawing*, in which ropes were bound around the head and twisted violently from side to side; and the *strappado*, in which the hands were tied behind the back, attached to a pulley and the whole body lifted off the ground. While in this position the body was often violently jerked or weights were attached to the feet, usually resulting in the arms being pulled out of their sockets. One of the most horrific instruments was known as the *boots*, or the *bootikens*, and consisted of a pair of iron leg braces that were gradually tightened with successive blows of a hammer, crushing the shins and calves, often until they were reduced to little more than a pulp.

Destroying the legs in such a way should, of course, have been illegal but the list of illegally used tortures doesn't stop there. Many horrific accounts survive of mutilation and unimaginable suffering at the hands of sadistic and brutal torturers. Failure to control the use of torture often led to victims being subjected to just about anything their torturers cared to inflict. Alcohol was poured over the skin and set alight; eyes were gouged out; ears cut off; breasts and genitals mutilated. One well-known case of torture was that of Dr Fian, the Scottish witch accused of plotting to murder King James VI, whose agonising experiences were reported in a contemporary pamphlet called the *Newes From Scotland* in 1591:

His nails upon all his fingers were riven and pulled off with an instrument called in Scottish a Turkas, which in England we call a pair of pincers, and under every nail there was thrust in two needles over even up to the heads. At all which torments notwithstanding, the Doctor never shrank in any way; neither would he then confess it the sooner, for all the tortures inflicted upon him. Then was he with all convenient speed, by commandment, conveyed again to the torment of the boots, wherein he continued a long time, and did abide so many blows in them, that his legs were crushed and beaten together as small as might be; and the bones and flesh so bruised, that the blood and marrow spurted forth in great abundance; whereby, they were made unserviceable for ever.

Dr Fian refused to confess to the last. It was a common belief about witches that the Devil helped them to withstand torture in the same way God helped the innocent. The Devil's apparent assistance in helping his witches endure torture was routinely used as an excuse to inflict ever greater suffering on defendants in an effort to force their confessions. The conviction rate in continental witchcraft trials was around 95%, as defendants were almost guaranteed to confess anything their captors wanted to hear. In England, by contrast, where torture was only permitted in cases of treason, the conviction rate for witchcraft was only around 50%. Confessions were used as evidence of the existence of witchcraft not only inside the courtrooms but outside them as well. The apparent willingness of alleged witches to confess under torture seemed to their persecutors to serve as confirmation of the reality of their crimes and ultimately helped to perpetuate and disseminate the belief in witchcraft.

In regions where the Inquisition remained strong, notably Italy and Spain, witchcraft trials were actually far less frequent than in other areas. Unlike many localised secular courts, which often acted with relative impunity and a large degree of independence, the Inquisition was a centrally controlled and strictly regulated body. For this reason incidents of the illegal use of torture and other miscarriages of justice were far less likely to be tolerated, and the Inquisition's considerable experience in dealing with heretics taught inquisitors to be far more cautious in accepting the reliability of evidence extracted under torture. In short, despite its fearsome reputation, the Inquisition often proved to be far less brutal than its secular equivalents.

The Hammer of Witches

In 1486 the Dominican inquisitors for Upper Germany, Jacob Sprenger and Heinrich Krämer (also known by his Latin name of Institoris) produced a handbook for witch finders known as *Malleus Maleficarum*, the 'Hammer of Witches'. It styled itself on earlier inquisitors' manuals for hunting down heretics, and contained a detailed compendium of learned witch beliefs as well as instructions on the legal procedures recommended for prosecuting suspected witches. It has entered into history as one of the most influential texts of European witch-hunting and was referred to repeatedly by later witch-hunters, both Catholic and Protestant, throughout the centuries following its first publication.

Sprenger and Krämer had been constantly frustrated in their efforts to hunt down witches by their local German hosts, who were none too keen on their activities. They turned for assistance to Pope Innocent VIII and, in 1484, he obliged them with a papal letter, *Summis Desiderantes*, the 'Witch Bull', in which he criticised the obstructive German locals and sanctioned Sprenger and Krämer's judicial operation against witches:

> It has recently come to our ears, not without great pain to us, that in some parts of Upper Germany ... many persons of both sexes, heedless of their own salvation and

forsaking the catholic faith, give themselves over to devils male and female, and by their incantations, charms and conjurings . . . ruin and cause to perish the offspring of women, the foal of animals, the products of the earth, the grapes of vines, and the fruit of trees . . . And, although our beloved sons Henricus Institoris and Jacobus Sprenger . . . have been and still are deputed by our apostolic letters as inquisitors of heretical pravity . . . certain of the clergy and of the laity of those parts, seeking to be wise above what is fitting . . . do not blush obstinately to assert that . . . it is illicit for the aforesaid inquisitors to exercise their office of inquisition . . . and that they ought not to be permitted to proceed to punishment, imprisonment, and correction of the aforesaid persons for the offences and crimes above named.

To reinforce the papal authority of their work Sprenger and Krämer reproduced the Witch Bull as a preface to the *Malleus Maleficarum*, and also included, in an appendix, a document apparently conferring the support of the faculty of theology at the University of Cologne. At least part of this document has now been exposed as a forgery. The *Malleus* was mainly the work of Krämer, who seems to have been somewhat mentally unbalanced and exhibited a profound hatred of women. A good deal of the *Malleus* is given over to the discussion of women's natural predisposition to evil and their susceptibility to the crime of witchcraft, as well as lurid descriptions of sexual relations between witches and demons and much prurient discussion of the nature of these unions:

There is also, concerning witches who copulate with devils, much difficulty in considering the methods by which such abominations are consummated. On the part of the devil: first, of what element the body is made he assumes; secondly, whether the act is always accompanied by the injection of semen received from another; thirdly, as to time and place, whether he commits this act more frequently at one time than at another; fourthly, whether the act is invisible to any who may be standing by.

Krämer's sordid preoccupations and over-zealous methods were to lead to a great deal of criticism of him from within his own ranks. In 1490, the Dominican order condemned him and even Sprenger parted company with him. The Bishop of Innsbruck is reported to have called Krämer 'completely childish' and, in 1485, released from prison around 50 suspected witches whom Krämer had incarcerated there.

The *Malleus* did not have anything new to say about witchcraft but it was the first comprehensive statement on the subject to gather together the many newly emerged ideas on it and structure them into one orderly theory, complete with 'appropriate' legal responses. It represents the first systematic approach towards the formalisation of the classic witchcraft stereotype. As such, in its role as a sort of 'encyclopaedia' of witch beliefs, it became influential in forming the attitudes and opinions of the majority of later witch-hunters and it also acted as a single source book for the extensive dissemination of those beliefs. There is, however, no evidence to suggest that the *Malleus* directly triggered any widespread outbreaks of witch-hunting in the years following its initial publication. Rather, it seems to have served as part of the consciousness-raising process by which the learned witch beliefs of the élite gradually trickled down to the rest of society and began to instil in the general population a sense of fear and anxiety about the diabolical activities of witches and the need to take action against them.

Voices of Opposition

As the disapproval of Krämer's fanaticism demonstrates, support for witch-hunting was far from universal and critics certainly did exist, even amongst the priesthood. But speaking out against witch-hunts often proved to be a dangerous activity. The Renaissance doctor Johann Weyer courted the outrage of many of his contemporaries, including Jean Bodin who accused him of being a witch after Weyer condemned the belief in witchcraft in 1563. In 1519 the influential occult philosopher Henry Cornelius Agrippa had also risked his own life to defend a woman successfully against charges of witchcraft. In the process he also succeeded in discrediting the brutal methods of Nicholas Savin, who was the inquisitor for the German town of Metz, where Agrippa held the post of advocate.

A peasant woman from the nearby village of Vuoypy was accused of witchcraft by her neighbours and brought before Savin. The neighbours gave Savin gifts of cake and dairy products and the judge who was assisting him, John Leonard, received a gift of gold coins. Agrippa became extremely concerned about the nature of the proceedings but, when he tried to voice his concerns about the infringement of the woman's legal rights, he was thrown out of the courtroom and accused of sympathising with a heretic. Savin then persuaded the villagers to take the accused woman back to Vuoypy where he and Leonard heard the case together in a trial that was not only illegal but also outside Leonard's jurisdiction. Taking his cue from the *Malleus Maleficarum*, Savin had the woman tortured but the court officials appointed as questioners were so disturbed at what they witnessed that they hastily departed in horror, leaving the woman entirely at Savin's mercy. Savin and his torturer brutalised the woman and left her without food or water. Then events took an unexpected turn. Judge Leonard fell fatally ill. While he lay dying, Leonard was plagued with doubts about what he and Savin had done and became convinced of the woman's innocence. He wrote to Savin, begging for her release, but to no avail. Upon Leonard's death, Agrippa continued to press for the woman's rights and wrote to Leonard's replacement, fiercely rebuking Savin's actions:

... brother Nicholas Savin, of the Dominican convent, Inquisitor of heretics, has fraudulently dragged into his slaughterhouse this innocent woman, contrary to Christian conscience, brotherly kindness, contrary to sacerdotal custom, the profession of his rule, the form of laws and canons: and has also, as a wicked man, wickedly and wrongfully exposed her to atrocious and enormous torments ...

Agrippa's intervention saved the woman and she was absolved. Her neighbours were fined for having wrongly accused her and Nicholas Savin fell into disgrace. But Agrippa's stand against the power and might of the

Inquisition brought him a dangerous notoriety. He was already known as a magician and alchemist and now his position in Metz became so precarious that he was forced to resign his post and flee to the relative safety of Cologne.

Doubt and Decline

If the legal system was largely responsible for facilitating the rise in witch-hunting, then it was also ultimately responsible for its eventual decline. The dawn of the Age of Enlightenment and the advent of Cartesian Rationalism provoked in Europe's learned élite a new sense of scepticism and provided the first real ideological challenge to the dominance of medieval scholasticism. This new scepticism certainly played an important role in bringing prosecutions to an end but it was mainly the growth of the legal arguments against witch-hunting, rather than the ideological arguments against the belief in witchcraft itself, that were instrumental in bringing about the beginning of the end of the Witch Craze.

Central to the growing legal case against witchcraft in the late seventeenth and early eighteenth centuries was the question of the reliability of the evidence. Large chain-reaction hunts had by now spun out of control on so many occasions that people began seriously to doubt the validity of the mechanisms being used to locate and prosecute suspected witches. Many communities found their very social fabric torn apart as scores of clearly innocent people were being sucked in and implicated in the alleged diabolical plots. Judges began to demand far greater proof that a crime had actually been committed before they were prepared to blame witchcraft, and many types of evidence that had previously been admissible were now being ruled out. The Devil's Mark, long accepted as one of the main pieces of evidence against the accused, was gradually ruled inadmissible by an increasing number of judges during the seventeenth century. So too was the 'spectral' evidence of those claiming to be magically afflicted by the disembodied spectre of the accused.

It was also now becoming increasingly clear to many that terrified and abused defendants were confessing to just about anything under torture and that the brutal methods used to extract these confessions were causing far too many miscarriages of justice. Torture had long been controversial for obvious humanitarian reasons but, during the seventeenth century, many states began to tighten their regulations concerning its application in an attempt to stamp out widespread misuse. One of those who became vocal in the call for the abolition of torture was Friedrich von Spee, a Jesuit priest who had been a fervent supporter of witchcraft trials. The Duke of Brunswick had been so horrified by the barbarism of torture that he outlawed its use throughout his lands and jurisdiction. He deliberately set a trap for Spee in which he had a suspected witch tortured in Spee's presence in such a way as to induce the woman to confess that she not only attended the Sabbat but that she had also seen Spee and another priest there as well. Spee and his fellow Jesuit had, according to the woman's confession, turned themselves into animals and engaged in sexual inter-course with the witches, who all gave birth to bizarre creatures with toads' heads and spiders' legs. Spee was so deeply shocked by what he witnessed that he became an ardent campaigner against the use of torture and, in 1631, anonymously published the influential *Cautio Criminalis*, exposing the unreliability of torture and cautioning prosecutors against its use.

Growing scepticism, both legal and ideological, found its eventual expression in the passing of new legislation across many European states in the late seventeenth and early eighteenth centuries, redesignating the crime of witchcraft as a non-capital offence and one that was increasingly regarded by many enlightened statesmen as the product of mere superstition and ignorance. However, by the time most of these new laws were actually passed, witch-hunting had already died out in many areas and the changes in legislature often had very little real impact on the decline of witch-hunting as a result. The use of torture was also eventually abolished but, once again, this often tended to occur in most areas long after its use in practice had actually ceased.

6

WITCHCRAFT IN BRITAIN AND THE COLONIES

England

Whilst wild sabbatic orgies raged across the Continent, witchcraft in England was an altogether quieter affair. Witch trials were fewer and quite different in character and content from their European cousins. English witches were generally not thought to fly to Sabbats, engage in perverted orgies or feast on babies' flesh. In fact, there were very few Sabbats to speak of compared with those on the Continent, although English witches sometimes attended a rather civilised meal with the Devil instead. For the most part, English witches were accused of simple *maleficia* such as causing disease and death, destroying crops and harming their neighbours or their neighbours' livestock. English witches were also usually found in the company of a familiar who would help them perform their evil acts in return for a drop of blood or milk.

The continental witchcraft stereotype never really reached English shores intact. England's identity on the periphery of Europe remained culturally and ideologically distinct from many of its European neighbours. The medieval heretics, and the Inquisition that accompanied them, had little impact in England and witchcraft never really developed into the full-blown conspiracy theory that spread terror across the Continent. Even the *Malleus Maleficarum* was not translated into English until relatively modern times, although it enjoyed scores of reprints on the Continent.

More prominent in cases of English, and also Scottish, witchcraft than some of the continental ideas was the prevalence of traditional British folk beliefs concerning the Faeries, or Good People, as they were often known (not to be confused with the tiny gossamer-winged Tinkerbells of Victorian fantasy). Belief in the witch's familiar in particular is closely associated with the belief that witches consorted with and received assistance from the Faeries, and many of the familiar spirits, devils and demons named in trial records are either directly referred to as being of Faery origin or contain elements of Faery belief overlaid with a thin veneer of Christian demonology. Alongside this belief in the Faery familiar went the learned belief in the Pact, and the idea that it must necessarily follow that, in order for the Faeries to have offered their assistance, the witch must have renounced Christ and offered up her soul in exchange.

English laws passed against witchcraft testify to the fact that English witches never fully lost their original association with sorcery and *maleficia*. The main body of law passed against witchcraft in England deals almost entirely with the ill effects of enchantments, conjurations and simple sorceries rather than with heresy and diabolical pacts. Witchcraft was treated as a secular matter and trials were usually held at the county assizes. The relative leniency with which England viewed the crime of witchcraft extended to the death penalty, which was carried out by hanging rather than burning. Furthermore, torture was only legally permissible in cases of treason.

The first statute against witchcraft in England was passed in 1542, during the reign of Henry VIII. The bill 'against conjurations and witchcrafts and sorcery and enchantment' outlawed the use of magic to discover the whereabouts of buried treasure hidden under old stone crosses, an 'infinite number' of which had apparently been subjected to vandalism and had been 'digged up and pulled down ... within this Realm'. The statute also outlawed love charms and causing harm 'through witchcrafts, enchantments or sorceries'. The penalty for these crimes was to be forfeiture of property and death. The new law remained largely unused, however, and it was repealed in 1547, during the reign of Edward VI. Another law was passed in 1563, this time under the daughter of Henry VIII, Elizabeth I. Elizabeth's bill 'against conjurations, enchantments and witchcrafts' restored much of her father's statute, although it called for a year's imprisonment for a first offence and the death penalty only after a second offence.

One of the first trials to take place under the new Elizabethan law occurred in 1566 at Chelmsford in

Essex. In many ways, the trial is characteristic of a typical English witch trial, containing as it does many accusations that may seem absurd to the modern observer. Agnes Waterhouse, her daughter Joan, and Elizabeth Francis were initially accused of various acts of *maleficia* but Elizabeth Francis then also confessed to receiving from her grandmother a cat that went by the name of Satan who was said to be, as his name suggested, none other than the Devil himself. Elizabeth said she had been taught to suckle the cat with her own blood, as well as some bread and milk, and, in return, Satan had helped her out by despatching a lover who refused to marry her, as well as her unborn child and her infant daughter. Elizabeth later decided to give Satan to Agnes Waterhouse. When she had to go away for a while, Agnes became concerned about who would look after Satan in her absence. After discussing the problem with Satan they both agreed that it would be far more convenient if the cat were to transform himself into a toad so that Agnes could keep him in a small wooden box with the minimum of fuss.

When Joan Waterhouse went to her mother's house to call upon Satan for his help he appeared to her, this time in the form of a large, shaggy black dog. Joan's main accuser, a twelve-year-old girl, claimed that Satan had appeared to her in this form, at the request of Joan, and had taunted and teased her before stealing the key to the dairy. Joan vigorously refuted the girl's allegations, pointing out that the girl had described the dog as having a face like an ape, and that therefore they could not possibly both be talking about the same dog. Agnes and Elizabeth were both found guilty and Agnes was hanged;

her daughter Joan was found not guilty. Elizabeth was hanged some years later after a second offence.

The most prominent voice of reason arguing against the belief in witchcraft in sixteenth-century England was that of Reginald Scot and his views were favourably received by many English clerics. In 1584, Scot published *The Discoverie of Witchcraft*, in which he pilloried the belief in witchcraft, called for an end to the terrible injustices caused by the prosecution of innocent old women and denounced the Catholic Church for creating witches out of the poor while canonising the rich. He described in detail the common folklore and superstition that fuelled belief in witchcraft and supported Johann Weyer's position that those who believed themselves to be witches were suffering from delusions caused by mental imbalance. He also identified certain other witches who were truly malevolent and could harm people by poisoning (but not by supernatural means) and others still who were merely frauds, taking money from the desperate and gullible. However, Scot denied completely the efficacy of both the Devil's power and the witches' magic.

James VI of Scotland ascended the English throne in 1603 as James I of England and, although it is not clear whether James had a direct hand in framing it or not, a new law against witchcraft was passed by parliament in 1604. The new law remained in place until 1735, when witchcraft ceased to be a capital offence in England. The 1604 law tightened Elizabeth's law by calling for the death penalty after the first offence if harm had been caused through magical means or if a corpse had been exhumed for magical purposes. Divining for hidden treasure also now carried a life sentence. As king of Scotland James had travelled to Denmark to collect his bride-to-be and it is probable that he was exposed to continental ideas about witchcraft during his stay, bringing them back to Scotland with him. During his reign in Scotland, James took a keen interest in witch-craft and encouraged prosecutions. In 1597, enraged by Reginald Scot's sceptical position, he even published *Daemonologie*, his own work on the subject, refuting Scot's views and, on his ascension to the English throne, he ordered copies of Scot's book to be publicly burned. But, as he grew older, James became increasingly sceptical about the reality of witchcraft. In 1616, he even intervened to halt a trial in Leicester while on a brief visit to the town. Nine witches had already gone to the gallows during the case and another six were in prison, about to be brought to trial. The main prosecution witness was a boy of around twelve years of age, and James demanded that the boy be brought before him for questioning. He dismissed the boy as a fraud and immediately ordered the release of the remaining prisoners. He also reprimanded the judge involved in the case for accepting such unreliable and dubious evidence.

The first major trial to take place under the new law of 1604 was in Lancashire in 1612, and this was the first English trial to depict witches flying on broomsticks in the continental style. Two old women with a reputation for sorcery in the Pendle Forest area of Lancashire, known as Old Demdike and Old Chattox, were charged, together with Old Demdike's granddaughter, Alison Device. They were alleged to have fallen into a dispute with a local miller and to have bewitched to death his daughter in revenge. Old Demdike confessed to having been lured into the Devil's service many years earlier, after he appeared to her one day in the form of a small boy wearing a coat that was half black and half brown. He gave his name as 'Tibb' and later appeared to her as a brown dog and sucked blood from her armpit, causing her to run mad for several months afterwards. After the arrests around 21 family members and supporters met for a meal one night and apparently hatched a daring plot to break the women out of Lancaster castle using gunpowder. Before they could act, however, the judge got wind of the plot and had most of them arrested and charged as well. One by one, they began to testify against each other and, in the end, ten people were sent to the gallows. Old Demdike died in prison before her trial began.

In 1633, another of Old Demdike's granddaughters, Jennet Device, was involved in the second famous witch trial to occur in the Pendle Forest area. Edmund Robinson, a local farmer's son of around ten years of age, claimed that he had come across two greyhounds while out one day and that, when they refused to chase a hare for him, he began to beat them. Suddenly they transformed themselves into a young boy and a local woman, Mother Dickenson, who tried to entice Edmund into the Devil's service. When Edmund refused, the boy transformed himself into a horse and Mother Dickenson grabbed Edmund, jumped up onto the horse and made off across the countryside. She eventually alighted at a barn and took Edmund inside, where Edmund claimed a witches' Sabbat was under way, attended by 50 or more witches. Edmund watched as they tucked into a grand feast that was lowered from the ceiling of the barn on ropes. Edmund affected his escape and, encouraged by his father, reported the whole matter to the local authorities. Edmund claimed, however, that he could only identify most of the witches by sight, and he was given leave to travel around the local parishes pointing out the witches. He received a fee for every positive ID and quickly ran up a total of over 30 witches, including Mother Dickenson and Jennet Device. Suspecting that financial reward might be at the root of Edmund's eagerness, the local authorities decided to refer the whole affair to the Bishop of Chester who soon uncovered evidence that Edmund's father had been accepting bribes from some of the accused to prevent the boy from testifying against them. Edmund's father admitted that he had ordered his son to make up the whole story in order to make money and he was sent to jail in place of the accused.

The one name that is, perhaps, associated with English witchcraft more than any other is that of Matthew Hopkins, the notorious 'Witch-Finder General'. Hopkins was the son of a puritan minister from Suffolk. His early career as a lawyer failed to make much of an impact and, in 1644, he embarked on a new career as the self-styled Witch-Finder General. Hopkins claimed to hold a commission from parliament (something which has never been proven) and set about ridding East Anglia of its witches with a degree of ruthlessness that eventually led to his downfall and disgrace several years later. Over a two-year period, Hopkins was responsible for more executions for witchcraft than had taken place throughout England over the whole of the previous century. Records are incomplete but the estimated tally of his victims stands at over 100.

In the chaos of Civil War England, Hopkins, along with his associate John Stearne and their select team of assistants, travelled from town to town in the counties of Essex and Suffolk, terrorising the inhabitants and charging huge sums of money for their services. On the basis of his alleged commission from parliament, Hopkins is said on one occasion to have ordered town officials to levy a special tax on the townsfolk in order to pay his exorbitant expenses of £28, a colossal sum of money in seventeenth-century England. It is quite possible that this was also his *modus operandi* in many of the other towns he visited.

Although physically torturing his victims was illegal, Hopkins specialised in a whole range of cruel techniques that kept him just inside the law. The majority of his victims were poor, elderly women. Suspects were stripped and searched for evidence of witch marks, starved and deprived of sleep for two or three days at a time, forced to sit cross-legged and bound into position with rope for periods of a day or more with no food or sleep, or continuously walked up and down until their feet bled, again for days at a time with no food or sleep. Hopkins was also well known for the public spectacle of *swimming* suspected witches. The swimming of witches was a throwback to the feudal concept of trial by water, in which the accused was thrown into water to see if she would sink to the bottom (innocent) or float (guilty). The belief was widely held that water, which was God's element, would naturally reject a witch.

Swimming was the favoured method of King James I in his *Daemonologie*, which Hopkins referred to throughout his witch-hunting career. The accused had their arms crossed over their knees and their thumbs tied to their toes and were then cast into the water while attached to a rope. Whether and how far they sank may well have been largely dependent on who was in control of the other end of the rope.

In his 1647 book, *The Discoverie of Witches*, Hopkins recounts how he was prompted to launch his crusade against witchcraft while living in the Essex town of Manningtree. He became convinced that a group of local witches was meeting regularly at a house nearby, where they sacrificed to the Devil and conversed with their familiars. Hopkins took it upon himself to have a one-legged old woman called Elizabeth Clarke arrested and, after four days without sleep, Clarke gave in and confessed, naming her accomplices. At the very moment of her confession, Hopkins claimed, the room briefly filled one by one with a group of Clarke's impish familiars, as she called for them each by name. One of his assistants later swore in court that he too had witnessed the apparitions. In total the Manningtree hunt resulted in 23 deaths, 19 at the gallows and another four in prison.

Hopkins was not, by any stretch of the imagination, a universally popular figure and his methods led to widespread public disapproval and backlash. In 1645, he was ordered to cease the practice of swimming witches and tradition has it that he was himself seized by an angry mob and subjected to swimming. He floated. After increasing controversy he was forced into retirement in 1646 and seems to have died, in disgrace, the following year.

Scotland

The number of witches executed in Scotland was three times higher than that in England, a country four times Scotland's size. Scotland's more receptive attitude towards European ideas made the Continental stereotype of the witch more widely accepted than in England and the country's Calvinist ministers, who sat in the General Assembly, were certainly more keen to press for the persecution of witches than their more reserved English counterparts. The Witchcraft Act of 1563 was harsher than its English equivalent and called for the death penalty for all those convicted, although a capital sentence wasn't always carried out. Unlike in England, torture was regularly used, although often illegally. Convicted witches were usually burnt, although they were generally strangled first. In 1590 King James VI of Scotland decided to appoint royal commissions to hunt down witches but, by 1597, the year in which his *Daemonologie* was published, James was beginning to have doubts about the widespread prosecution of witches, over which he was able to exercise little central control, and he revoked the royal commissions. He stipulated instead that the Privy Council must first examine the evidence in all cases of suspected witchcraft before a trial could be authorised.

Probably the most famous case of witchcraft in Scottish history involved no less than King James VI himself and his 'half-mad cousin' Francis, fifth Earl of Bothwell. The case became known as that of the 'North Berwick witches' and Bothwell was accused of conspiring with them to assassinate the king. The seeds of this royal intrigue were sown many years earlier during the reign of King James V. During his marriage to Mary of Guise, James V only managed to produce one child, a daughter, later to become Mary, Queen of Scots. He fared much better however with his string of mistresses, with whom he produced three illegitimate sons, John, James and Robert Stewart. The three were eventually legitimised in 1551 and John Stewart married Lady Jean Hepburn, sister of the fourth Earl of Bothwell, who was the second husband of Mary, Queen of Scots. When the fourth Earl died insane in a Danish prison in 1576, John Stewart's son Francis was made the fifth Earl. Francis inherited estates including Dumfries, Kirkcudbright, Lanark, Selkirk, Berwickshire and North Berwick. Very much like his father before him, he was variously described as 'daring, powerful and unprincipled', 'the oppressor of honest men', 'a wilful murderer' and the 'relentless persecutor' of James VI, whose throne he coveted.

On 10 August 1593 Bothwell was put on trial in Edinburgh:

> Francis Earl of Bothwell hath been detected of witch-craft, and if any such thing may be proved against him he is here to endure the law; if not, such as have been his accusers shall be accounted as evil members and seditious persons of the commonwealth and so shall be reported.

Despite the fact that these 'accusers' had already been put to death, the trial went ahead anyway. The panel of judges was mostly made up of Bothwell's friends and fellow noblemen and he hired the best defence lawyer in the country. Just to be on the safe side, he also packed Edinburgh's streets with his own private army.

The diabolical conspiracy had been uncovered, apparently by accident, when the deputy bailiff of the town of Tranent, David Seaton, began to suspect that his maid possessed miraculous powers of healing. Gillie Duncan would absent herself from her master's house each night and go about the town performing marvellous acts of healing on the sick. Seaton felt that there could only be one possible explanation for Duncan's abilities: she was in league with the Devil and it was he who had given her the power to heal. Seaton questioned Duncan but, when she failed to explain herself adequately, he began to torture her. He crushed her fingers in the pinniewinks and thrawed her head but to no avail. Next he began to search for the Devil's Mark, which he duly discovered on her throat. At this point Duncan gave in and confessed, naming a list of accomplices.

Among those named by Duncan and subsequently arrested were the schoolmaster at Saltpans, Dr Fian (also known as John Cunningham) and a 'grave and matron-like woman of rank' from Nether Keith called Agnes Sampson who was well known as a midwife and often referred to as the Wise Wife of Keith. Two respectable and high-ranking ladies of Edinburgh were also accused: Euphemia Maclean, the daughter of Lord Cliftonhall and a very wealthy woman in her own right, and Barbara Napier, the sister-in-law of the Laird of Carshogle and 'reputed as civil and honest as any in Edinburgh'. Others named by Duncan included Margaret Thompson (sometimes referred to as Agnes Thompson of Edinburgh), the skipper Robert Grierson, the wife of David Seaton's porter, and 'innumerable others in those parts'.

Agnes Sampson was brought before the king but would not confess. She was taken away and searched for the Devil's Mark which was found on her genital area. The old woman was then tortured and forced to wear a Witch's Bridle, before finally confessing. Most of the 53 counts against her were related to healing the sick, but Sampson also confessed to attending the Sabbat. The description of the witches' revels that Sampson is alleged to have given is vividly recounted in the *Newes From Scotland* in 1591:

> ... upon Allhallows Eve last, she was accompanied ... with a great many other witches, to the number of two hundred: and that all together went by sea each one in a riddle or sieve ... with flagons of wine making merry and drinking by the way ... to the Church of North Berwick in Lothian, and that after they had landed, took hands on the land and danced back-to-back ... the Devil being then at North Berwick Church attended their coming in the habit or likeness of a man, and seeing that they tarried over long, he at their coming enjoined them all to a penance, which was, that they should kiss his buttocks, in sign of duty to him: which being put on the pulpit bare, every one did as he had enjoined them: and having made his ungodly exhortations, wherein he did greatly inveigh against the king of Scotland, he received their oaths for their good and true service towards him ...

King James VI, however, was not at all convinced about the veracity of the witches' confessions and called them all 'extreme lyars'. In order to convince the king that she was telling the truth, Sampson is said to have approached him and, in hushed tones, repeated to him the private conversation that had taken place between himself and his bride on their wedding night. She then revealed the various plots hatched by the witches to kill him.

According to her account, Sampson met with Gillie Duncan and Dr Fian at the weaver's house, where they baptised a cat that had been supplied to them by the Devil. They then attached human toe and finger bones to each of the poor creature's four paws and cast it into the sea (the cat is said to have been less than impressed and promptly swam ashore unharmed). This was done, Sampson said, to raise a storm that would sink the king's boat as he sailed to Norway to bring back his bride, Anne of Denmark. Her ship had been caught in severe storms as it attempted to leave Norway for Scotland in 1589 and she became stranded at Oslo. James sailed out to meet her but the terrible storms prevented the pair from leaving Norway until the following spring. Sampson is alleged to have said that 'the said christened cat was the cause', and that 'his Majesty had never come safely from the Sea, if his faith had not prevailed above their [the witches] intentions'.

The witches had failed to prevent the king and his bride from reaching dry land but two more attempts on his life were made. Firstly, Agnes Sampson carved a waxen image of the king. Attempts were made to acquire some piece of the king's clothing in which to wrap the image but nothing was procured. The waxen image was then given over to the Devil to enchant and was later thrown upon the fire by Euphemia Maclean and Barbara Napier in an effort to destroy the king himself. The second enchantment involved the use of a toad. Dr Fian took the toad to Barbara Napier's house, where they

roasted it and then hung it up over an oyster shell to
catch the drips. To this toad juice was added the skin of
an adder, some urine, and 'the thing in the forehead of a
new-foaled foal'. This foul brew was to be 'laid in his
majesty's way . . . that it might drop upon his highness'
head, or his body, for his highness' destruction'. Again,
neither attempt proved successful.

The alleged leader of the North Berwick witches was
Dr Fian, the Saltpans schoolmaster, who was described
as 'nothing less than a Scottish Dr Faustus'. Fian was
charged with 20 counts of witchcraft, including swearing
an oath of allegiance to the Devil and acting as secretary,
or Regester, at the witches' meetings, as well as plotting
to murder the king. The *Newes From Scotland* declared
of Fian that:

> . . . the examination of his acts since his apprehension,
> declareth the great subtletie of the Devil, and therefore
> maketh things to appear the more miraculous; for being
> apprehended by the accusation of the said Gillie Duncan
> aforesaid, who confessed he was their Regester, and that
> there was not one man suffered to come to the Devil's
> readings but only he [i.e. he was the only male tolerated
> at the 'readings'].

After his failure to confess, Fian was brutally tortured.
The *Newes From Scotland* records how, after a spell in
the Boots, Fian had still not confessed. The other witches
suggested that his gaolers should look under his tongue,
where they duly discovered two pins, embedded deep
into his mouth. According to the other witches, this was
a charm to prevent him from confessing. After the

removal of the pins, Fian was taken before the king where he confessed, renouncing the Devil and promising to become a good Christian. He was taken back to his cell and the next day complained to his gaolers that the Devil had appeared to him during the night and demanded that he not break his pact. By the following morning Fian had vanished, having apparently found the key to his cell and affected his escape.

His freedom was short-lived. He was soon discovered at Saltpans and rearrested. Upon his return to prison, Fian enraged the king by retracting his previous confession. James became convinced that Fian had, during his absence, renewed his contract with the Devil and ordered that he be searched for a new Devil's Mark. No kind of mark could be found and Fian was subjected to the most horrendous bout of torture. Needles were driven in under his fingernails and the nails pulled out with a pair of pincers, then his legs were crushed to a pulp in the Boots, 'whereby they were made unserviceable forever'. But Fian defiantly refused to confess anything, saying only that he had been forced into his original confession 'for fear of pains which he had endured'. He was condemned to death and, in January 1591, he was taken to Castle Hill in Edinburgh, where he was *worried* (i.e. strangled) before being burnt.

Agnes Sampson was also worried and then burnt, but Euphemia Maclean was not so lucky and was *burnt quick*, that is burnt alive. Barbara Napier was taken to Castle Hill, where her stake had been prepared, but she was given a last minute reprieve because she was pregnant and it was felt to be irreligious to burn a pregnant woman.

The Earl of Bothwell's implication in the witches' plots was said to have taken the form of more than 20 clandestine meetings between his representative, Ninian Chirnside, and a notorious warlock called Richard Graham, whose name had cropped up in the confessions of Barbara Napier and Euphemia Maclean. Graham's alleged evidence, however, had been obtained under torture before his execution and Bothwell's defence quickly demolished its usefulness in a court of law, pointing out that, since he was a criminal and a witch, as well as an excommunicate, Graham's testimony was legally inadmissible. Bothwell agreed that he had had some slight dealings with Graham via Chirnside but these were entirely legitimate and wholly innocent. Bothwell was acquitted. After all, as one commentator has wryly observed, 'it would be a sorry day for the Scottish nobility, and a most unhappy precedent, if so slight a matter as conspiring against the monarch should be rewarded with the death penalty'.

Central to many Scottish witch trials was the belief in the Faeries, and many traditional elements of Faery lore figure in trial records. Encounters with the Faery queen, known as the Queen of Elphame, are often mentioned in confessions. On the Celtic fringes of Britain, the Faeries were often identified in popular folklore with the fallen angels who, it was believed, had been bound into the valleys of the earth until Judgement Day. Like the planet Venus, they were thought to be most often visible to humans at the 'betwixt and between' times of dusk and dawn. One of the most detailed confessions describing contact with the Faeries was that of Bessie Dunlop of Dalry in Ayrshire. Bessie described at length her meetings with a Faery man called Tom Reid who told her that the Queen of Elphame had sent him to wait upon her and help her. With his assistance, Bessie was able to heal the sick and recover stolen objects. Tom repeatedly asked Bessie to renounce the Catholic faith, but she steadfastly refused. She was convicted at the Edinburgh assizes on 8 November 1576 and most probably died at the stake.

One of the more mystifying episodes in the history of Scottish witchcraft involved what seemed to be the completely voluntary confession of Isobel Gowdie, an attractive young farmer's wife from Morayshire. One day, in April 1662, she came forward for no apparent reason and confessed to having been a witch since 1647. Gowdie astonished the authorities with her lengthy descriptions of diabolical activities and her confession is one of the most detailed accounts of witch beliefs and alleged practices ever recorded.

Gowdie claimed to have become a witch after meeting a man dressed in grey. She was baptised in her own blood by the Devil, given a mark and renamed Janet. Gowdie then joined a coven of 13 witches and learned her evil arts under the tutelage of the Faeries. The coven members flew to their Sabbats on beanstalks and straws of corn, where they engaged in feasting, wild dancing, and orgies with the Devil. Gowdie's description of sexual intercourse with the Devil was particularly lurid and detailed. His penis was huge and scaly and caused her excruciating pain; his semen was as cold as ice. Her husband, she claimed, never once noticed she was missing because she replaced herself in bed with a broomstick whenever she attended the Sabbat. Gowdie and her fellow witches often passed the time by blasting their neighbours' crops, raising storms and hexing people. They would attach tiny ploughs to toads and drive them across farmland to blight the crops, beat stones with wet rags to raise winds and stick dolls with pins or shoot people with 'elf arrows' to kill or injure them. Sometimes they would turn themselves into the likeness of a hare or a cat and go about the countryside.

Gowdie's confession introduced the word *coven* to describe congregations of witches and she explained the hierarchy and structure of the Scottish witch cult to which she claimed to belong. Dr Margaret Murray later used many of the details given by Gowdie in her thesis on the existence of a real witch cult which she believed was widespread throughout Europe. Gowdie's motives for confessing remain unknown.

Ireland

Witchcraft barely raised an eyebrow in Ireland and there are only a small handful of recorded trials. Ireland seems to have been even less receptive to Continental ideas about witchcraft than England and the few individual trials that took place in the centuries after Petronilla de Meath went to her death were concerned with alleged acts of sorcery and *maleficia*. A Witchcraft Act was passed in 1586 and, like the English acts, legislated against discovering buried treasure and causing harm with sorceries and enchantments. A rare case occurred in 1606 when a Protestant minister was charged with divining for hidden treasure and, in 1661, the 'Witch of Youghal', a woman named Florence Newton, was accused of bewitching a servant girl after kissing her.

After being sent to prison Florence was further accused of causing the death of a man, after kissing him too.

The first trial for witchcraft in Ireland was that of Lady Alice and her associates in 1324 and it is the one notable exception to Ireland's general indifference to witchcraft. The last trial to take place in Ireland was quite different from the first. It took place in Protestant Ulster in 1711 and was distinctly English in flavour. It was a basic case of bewitchment and had none of the trappings of European-style witchcraft that were evident in the case of Lady Alice some 400 years previously.

The strange events occurred in the small Presbyterian community of Island Magee, near Carrickfergus in Co. Antrim. Upon going to stay with her son and daughter-in-law in September 1710, the widow of a local minister, Mrs Hattridge, found herself plagued by frightening supernatural experiences. Each night as she lay in bed she was assaulted by an unseen force which threw stones and lumps of turf at her and tore the bedclothes from the bed. The terrified Mrs Hattridge moved to another room and the strange nocturnal occurrences abated.

One evening in December of that year, as Mrs Hattridge sat beside the fire, a small, scruffy boy suddenly appeared beside her. He said nothing and danced around the room before running off in the direction of the cattle shed, where he vanished. The boy did not appear again until February 1711, when he taunted and threatened the servants with a sword before digging a hole in the ground which he claimed was a grave 'for a corpse that will come out of this house very soon'. A few days later Mrs Hattridge again began to experience the unusual phenomena. Her clothes were moved about her room and the bedclothes were found formed into the shape of a corpse. She awoke in the middle of the night complaining of a terrible stabbing pain and, within a few days, Mrs Hattridge was dead.

A short time later, a new servant arrived at the house to act as a companion for the late Mrs Hattridge's daughter-in-law. But immediately upon her arrival Mary Dunbar also began to experience the strange and frightening phenomena. Her clothes were moved about and she collapsed in a fit and suffered seizures. It was Dunbar who brought the allegations of bewitchment, claiming that a group of local women was responsible for the terrifying events in the Hattridge household. Seven women named by Dunbar were arrested and brought to trial. Echoing events at Salem, Massachusetts, it was said that Dunbar fell into fits, suffering spectral visions of the accused, whenever one of them was brought near her. She was also reported to have vomited up large amounts of feathers, pins, buttons and yarns, and her seizures were often of such violence that she appeared to be choking.

At the short trial, which lasted only a matter of hours, Dunbar sat in a trance and was unable to speak, claiming that her tormentors would not allow her to testify against them. Judge Upton, presiding, was sceptical that Dunbar's afflictions, although clearly diabolical in origin, were being caused by the defendants. Upon inquiry he found that the accused were pious and industrious women and, most importantly, were all perfectly capable of reciting the Lord's Prayer without any trouble whatsoever, something that no witch under the Devil's power could possibly accomplish. Notwithstanding

their rather rough appearance, this was all the evidence
Judge Upton required to direct the jury to return a
verdict of not guilty. The jury, however, were of an
altogether different opinion, and all seven women were
found guilty. They were sentenced to a year in prison,
with quarterly appearances in the pillories, where it is
said that one of them was blinded in the eye by a cabbage
thrown at her.

New England

The puritan colony of New England experienced one of
the most notorious outbreaks of witch-hunting to take
place in the English-speaking world. This took place at
Salem village in Massachusetts in 1692. Although geo-
graphically remote from Europe, New England was still
very much a part of Europe, particularly in its cultural
outlook, and the puritan colonists carried the old
European witch beliefs with them into the New World,
along with an all-consuming fear of the Devil. There
were small sporadic outbreaks of witchcraft in the
colony from the 1640s onwards, but nothing to rival the
drama that occurred at Salem.

Salem village had suffered under the weight of
considerable political infighting for a good many years
when, in 1689, a controversial new minister, Samuel
Parris, arrived in the village. The witchcraft accusations
began after Betty Parris, the minister's nine-year-old
daughter, and Abigail Williams, his eleven-year-old
niece, began to dabble in the occult. The two girls were
joined by a number of other girls from the village and
they tried their hand at divination to foretell the
professions of their future husbands. In the process it

seems they succeeded in scaring themselves witless and, after a while, Betty Parris began suffering from convulsive fits and exhibiting bodily contortions and other strange behaviour. The other girls quickly followed suit and doctors, unable to fathom a cause, diagnosed bewitchment. In February 1692, the girls named three women as their tormentors.

The accused were Parris's West Indian slave Tituba and two other local women, Sarah Good and Sarah Osborne. Good and Osborne fervently denied the accusations but Tituba confessed enthusiastically, claiming that she was indeed a witch. According to Tituba's confession, there was a whole group of witches active in the area and it was led by a tall, white-haired man dressed in black who had made Tituba sign the Devil's book. Tituba had flown through the air to gatherings held by the witches, at which Good and Osborne were also present, and had been ordered to harm the girls by a large black dog. Tituba's willingness to confess may seem inexplicable or odd to the modern observer but it is likely she knew exactly what she was doing. Witches who confessed in New England were spared from the gallows and, in confessing, Tituba had been astute enough to save her own life. Parris and the town magistrates declared an all-out hunt and the three accused women were chained up in Boston jail, where the weak and elderly Osborne died.

The defendants could not actually be tried, however, because the colony had lost its right to try capital cases when its colonial charter was revoked during the Glorious Revolution of 1688 in England, in which William and Mary took the throne from James II. The loss of the charter had been taken as a sign by the colonists of God's punishment for sinning against him and it only served to increase their fears about the presence of evil in the colony. But the immediate lack of a trial did not stop the girls from continuing to name names. Soon many more people were denounced as witches and thrown into jail. The 'afflicted', as the girls became known, gained considerable notoriety and enormous power and what may have started out as a game for them quickly developed into something far more sinister.

In May 1692, the new governor of the colony finally arrived, bringing with him a new charter. Sir William Phips, more concerned with the unstable political climate and the military threat posed by the French and the Indians, took the unusual step of establishing a special Court of Oyer and Terminer (meaning 'to hear and determine') to deal with the huge backlog of witches as quickly as possible. Phips established a tribunal of distinguished jurors to hear the cases and promptly left to deal with more pressing military matters.

The girls were present in court throughout the proceedings and they would fall into convulsions, shrieking with pain and manifesting strange bite marks and bruises on their bodies each time one of the defendants was brought near, claiming they were being attacked by the spectres (disembodied spirits) of the accused. This spectral evidence was enough to convince the jurors of the guilt of the defendants and, on 10 June 1692, the first convicted witch was hanged. Another five were found guilty and hanged on 19 July, six more were hanged during August and, on 22 September, another eight met their deaths. The most unusual death, however, occurred not by hanging but by crushing. Giles Cory, an 80-year old farmer, refused to enter a plea of either innocent or guilty. He was taken out to the fields and subjected to an archaic English practice known as *peine forte et dure* (meaning 'strong and hard pain'). Cory was forced to lie down and a plank was laid across his chest; over a two-day period he was left there as more and more heavy stones were placed upon the plank, gradually crushing him. Cory defiantly refused to enter any kind of plea and, on 19 September, he died under the weight of the stones.

By the time proceedings were brought to a close, 185 people had been accused, 59 tried and 20 hanged. As with so many other trials on the European mainland at around this time, it was the questionable nature of the spectral evidence that ultimately led to concerns being voiced about the reliability of the verdicts. The ranks of the afflicted had grown to over 50 people and the entire affair had spun completely out of control. When Lady Phips herself was accused, the governor took decisive action and, on 29 October 1692, he dissolved the Court of Oyer and Terminer. The remaining defendants were tried in January 1693 at a specially established Superior Court; the spectral evidence of the afflicted was ruled inadmissible and, as a result, most of the accused were acquitted. The few that were found guilty were reprieved by governor Phips himself who refused to allow any more executions.

7

THE SEARCH FOR REAL WITCHES

Once the preserve of eccentrics, the study of witchcraft, after decades of hovering on the margins of respectable academia, has recently become more fashionable. The systematic modern study of the Witch Craze and its component parts has done much to help assemble the various pieces of the jigsaw puzzle that together create the larger picture of ideas, beliefs and motivations involved. Whilst much of the modern study of witchcraft has concerned itself with the elements that created the conditions in which the Witch Craze could flourish, some earlier scholars took a different approach and even put forward theories to suggest the existence of a real witch cult.

As early as 1749 the Italian scholar Girolamo Tartar-rotti-Serbiti ventured to suggest that the imagery and symbolism of the witches' Sabbat had its roots in ancient pagan beliefs. Jakob Grimm, in 1844, concurred and suggested that witch beliefs were the result of a fusion of popular ideas about pagan folklore and medieval heresy. Neither of these two men, however, actually believed there to have been a real witch cult. In 1828, a German law professor, Karl Ernst Jarcke, proposed that witches had been members of a surviving pagan cult that had gradually become so degraded by the influence of medieval Christianity that it finally degenerated into a Devil-worshipping sect. This thread was picked up a few years later by another German, Franz Josef Mone, who argued that witchcraft was a pre-Christian Greek import and was probably the relic of a mystery cult dedicated to Hecate or Dionysus. It was detested, he argued, by both homegrown patriotic German pagans and by later Christian authorities alike. Neither Jarcke nor Mone supported their arguments with any actual research or documentary evidence.

Michelet, Leland and the Victorian Radicals
By far the most influential theorist to enter the fray was Jules Michelet in 1862. In his popular bestseller, *La Sorcière*, Michelet hijacked witchcraft to suit his own radical political agenda and, in the process, created an enduring portrait of the witch as social rebel. Far from being a malevolent menace to medieval society, Michelet's witch had become a free-spirited, anti-establishment, pro-woman, pro-nature Romantic figure. Like Mone and Jarcke before him, Michelet disregarded the rigours of academic discipline and instead launched into a polemic against brutal medievalism and the absolute might of the sterile, misogynist Catholic Church, in which he championed the rebellious, egalitarian peasant.

Rather contrarily, Michelet asserted that the God of the witches was both the pagan nature god Pan and the Christian Devil. This Satan, however, was the ultimate rebel, the 'outlaw of outlaws', and the archetypal antihero. The witches who worshipped him were, for Michelet, the joyous defenders of freedom and the custodians of wild nature. Woman was the natural healer, the enchantress and keeper of ancient secrets handed down from mother to daughter across the generations.

Michelet's romanticised medieval peasant-witch encapsulated the spirit of nineteenth-century radicalism and inspired a number of later versions. One such version was that circulated by the American women's rights campaigner Matilda Joslyn Gage in the 1890s. It was she who first plucked the wildly inaccurate figure of nine million executions out of thin air and created one of the biggest historical misconceptions still in circulation today. Again, Gage did not attempt any serious research into her subject and, taking her cue from Michelet, she pitted her village wise woman against the powers of Church and State in a battle for the control of women's bodies, minds and souls. Like Michelet, Gage depicted her witch as the enemy of the establishment which was intent on reinforcing its masculine supremacy by suppressing the role of women as healers and rightful priestesses of a bygone matriarchal era that venerated Mother Earth. Gage's witch was later to resurface in radical pagan feminist discourse in the 1970s and entered into the mythology of the American Women's Movement as an icon of female power and knowledge.

The belief that witches were the last remnants of a prehistoric religion that elevated women and served the

Great Goddess became common currency amongst late nineteenth-century folklorists and neo-pagan Romantics. When the British Folk-Lore Society was formed in the 1890s, its president was only too happy to reinforce this popular view without the aid of any corroborative research or sound historical evidence.

The American folklorist Charles Godfrey Leland was the first to claim he had discovered actual evidence of a pre-Christian Dianic witch cult, still in existence in Italy at the end of the nineteenth century. He presented his evidence in the form of a manuscript he called the *Vangelo* or *Aradia, Gospel of the Witches*, which he claimed to have received from Italian witches via his local contact, a woman called Maddalena. Leland claimed his *Vangelo* set forth the beliefs and practices of *La Vecchia Religione*, or the Old Religion, as he had uncovered it in Tuscany. 'So long ago as 1886,' wrote Leland in 1890, 'I learned that there was in existence a manuscript setting forth the doctrines of Italian witchcraft, and I was promised that, if possible, it should be obtained for me.' Maddalena was dispatched to track down the document and, after repeated harrying by her employer, she eventually delivered a manuscript to him written in her own hand and purporting to be the very document he had so longed to procure.

The manuscript contains an assortment of stories, spells and incantations relating to the goddess Diana and her daughter Aradia, whose name is possibly a corruption of Herodias, St John the Baptist's New Testament nemesis, popularly associated with both Diana and her darker aspect Hecate. The first section of the *Vangelo* describes how Diana sent her daughter Aradia to earth to teach oppressed slaves and outlaws the art of sorcery and resistance, and how to pay homage to Diana at the Sabbat:

Whenever ye have need of anything,
Once in the month, and when the moon is full,
Ye shall assemble in some desert place,
Or in a forest all together join
To adore the spirit of your queen,
My mother, great Diana. She who fain
Would learn all sorcery yet has not won
Its deepest secrets, then my mother will
Teach her, in truth all things as yet unknown.
And ye shall all be freed from slavery,
And so ye shall be free in everything;
And as a sign that ye are truly free,
Ye shall be naked in your rites, both men
And women also: this shall last until
The last of your oppressors shall be dead;
And ye shall make the game of Benevento,
Extinguishing the lights, and after that
Shall hold your supper thus . . .

The authenticity of the manuscript has long been the subject of doubt. Leland was dismissed as an unreliable, even fraudulent, scholar by many of his contemporaries and Maddalena vanished shortly after the manuscript's appearance, prompting many to believe that her eagerness to please her employer is the most likely explanation for the *Vangelo*'s origin and contents. Like Michelet, Leland was a political radical who romanticised the simple rustic pleasures of country life and railed against the oppression of the peasantry. Some have suggested that his hand seems altogether too evident in many of the sentiments expressed in the *Vangelo* and he has been accused of either manufacturing his witch religion or of heavily doctoring the manuscript he received in order to fit his political outlook.

Margaret Murray

Perhaps the most famous and controversial attempt to prove the existence of an actual European witch cult was that of Egyptologist Dr Margaret Murray in her book *The Witch-Cult in Western Europe*, first published in the 1920s. Echoing the theories of the nineteenth-century folklorists before her, Murray argued that witches were not Devil worshippers at all but were, in fact, members of an organised pre-Christian fertility cult devoted to a pagan horned god called Dianus, the origins of which extended as far back as the Stone Age. This prehistoric cult, she argued, was organised into congregations known as *covens* and each coven consisted of 12 witches plus a Master, thought by outsiders to be the Devil, who was worshipped and revered by the witches as a divine incarnation of their god. As such, he presided over the Sabbat and was often dressed in animal skins and a horned mask to represent the ancient god of hunting and fertility.

Unlike her predecessors, Murray did her research and used actual trial evidence and the confessions of the accused to support her thesis. One of the major criticisms levelled against Murray is that she did not take into consideration the element of duress or psychological pressure involved in the extraction of these confessions but accepted the words of the alleged witches at face value and assumed that the confessions were actual descriptions of real events. Murray's rationalistic approach forced her to ignore the more fantastical elements of the confessions, such as night flight, and her theory was ultimately founded on a series of suppositions that simply didn't fit the evidence. The picture of witchcraft she relied on to construct her argument was drawn mostly from later trial evidence, which historians argue was the result of a composite of ideas and beliefs that took many centuries to reach maturity; it did not, they argue, pre-date Christianity, or even the Middle Ages, in the form Murray assumed it did.

It was just this kind of propensity to bend the facts to fit her theory that led to Murray being ridiculed and discredited. Perhaps, had she been more cautious in her assertions and made better use of her sources, her ideas may well have sparked a lively and intelligent debate within the academic community. As it was, she was dismissed as a crackpot and many historians, anxious to preserve their reputations, judiciously avoided the whole area of debate for many decades afterwards.

Ginzburg and the Benandanti

To date no reliable evidence has been uncovered to suggest that a real witch cult ever actually existed in any kind of widespread or organised form. Localised pagan beliefs clearly did exist, as did many people who practised magic of one form or another. Historians, it seems, have often been painstakingly piecing together the circumstances that generated the Witch Craze with the main piece of the puzzle, namely the witch herself, notable by her absence, or at least her silence. It is just this apparent silence that has preoccupied the renowned historian Carlo Ginzburg in recent years. Frustrated by many modern studies of the Witch Craze, which he believes have concentrated on studying the persecutors rather than the persecuted, Ginzburg has been inspired to ask just what it was that those accused of witchcraft actually believed about *themselves*. At least some of those accused of witchcraft clearly did believe that they actually took part in the crimes of which they were accused. Were these people mentally ill, as has been the standard response of many historians, or were there other layers of belief at work that have been previously ignored or overlooked? This question has led Ginzburg to examine the folk origins of many of the elements of the classic witchcraft stereotype and how they intersected with the beliefs of the learned élite.

Ginzburg has been bold enough to state that there may be at least a 'kernel of truth', as he puts it, in Margaret Murray's theories. Whilst Ginzburg believes Murray's theories to have been rightly discredited, he recognises that she did something that other historians have failed to do, that is, to look at the confessions of the accused, not from either the accuser's or the historian's point of view, but from the point of view of the accused themselves. Ginzburg was led to view Murray's work in this light following his discovery of some fascinating new evidence. Tucked away in the archives of the archbishop of Udine, in the Italian region of Friuli, Ginzburg uncovered evidence of a pagan fertility cult that existed during the sixteenth and seventeenth centuries. The members of this small agrarian cult were known as the *Benandanti*, 'good walkers' or 'well-farers', and were all born with a caul, which distinguished them from ordinary folk and marked them out for their special purpose in life. On certain nights of the year, usually on a Thursday night during the ember days, these Benandanti would leave their bodies and travel out in spirit to protect the crops from harm by doing battle with witches (known as the *Malandanti*) and evil spirits who were the enemies of fertility. When the Benandanti came to the attention of the Inquisition they affirmed their belief that they were the defenders of the Church against the evil doings of the witches. But there was simply no room in the inquisitors' worldview for a pagan cult that was beneficent and pro-fertility and, over a protracted period of decades, the inquisitors eventually managed to convince the Benandanti that they were, in fact, witches.

Ginzburg's discovery does *not* prove the existence of an organised, widespread witch cult, pagan or otherwise. There is no evidence that the Benandanti ever physically met together at nocturnal gatherings; their night journeys were purely spiritual and shamanic in nature. They also quite evidently believed themselves to be the enemies of the witches and concurred with the orthodox view that witches were the bringers of sterility and death. Despite the pagan origins of Benandanti beliefs, there is also no evidence that they ever actually *practised* any form of pagan religion and they often affirmed their faith in Christ. What Ginzburg's discovery does show us, however, is how these kinds of lingering pagan beliefs and customs could be taken by the inquisitors and misinterpreted as evidence of witchcraft. The same was probably true in the case of the trial of Pierina de Bugatis, in fourteenth-century Milan who was accused of attending the society of Signora Oriente. Ultimately, this was a clash of cultures. The inquisitors just couldn't understand how these Benandanti could magically travel out at night and *not* be witches. It flew in the face of everything they knew about witchcraft and was, after all, contrary to the teachings of the *Canon Episcopi*, which forbade belief in the night ride on the grounds that it was the 'error of the pagans' and should be regarded as a dangerous illusion caused by the Devil. 'Such phantasms,' states the *Canon Episcopi*, 'are imposed on the minds of infidels and not by the divine but by the malignant spirit.'

The ability of the inquisitors subtly to impose their learned witch beliefs upon the peasant Benandanti, to the point where the Benandanti became utterly convinced that they must be witches, is what Ginzburg refers to as a 'process of acculturation', and is something which could only have taken place over an extended period of time. 'The gap between the questions of the judges and the confessions of the accused,' writes Ginzburg, 'was gradually reduced only in the course of decades.' The beliefs of the Benandanti were, as Ginzburg observes, 'a stratum of popular beliefs which the inquisitors could only slowly make coincide with their own preconceived ideas'. What makes Ginzburg's work so important is that, because of the richness and extent of the documentary evidence uncovered, he has been able carefully to reconstruct this 'process of acculturation' from the point of view of the Benandanti themselves, and provide us with a microcosmic view of the gradual assimilation of paganism and folk belief into the dominant witch beliefs of the learned élite.

RESOURCES

Early Origins of the Devil
Many faiths share the story of the Garden of Eden, and the temptation of Adam and Eve. It can be found in Genesis, chapter 1 of the Bible, as well as the Koran (17. 61). In this account the fallen angel is called Iblis (see p. 11), as he defies Allah:

(17. 61) And when We said to the angels: Make obeisance to Adam; they made obeisance, but Iblis (did it not). He said: Shall I make obeisance to him whom Thou hast created of dust?

(17. 62) He said: Tell me, is this he whom Thou hast honored above me? If Thou shouldst respite me to the day of resurrection, I will most certainly cause his progeny to perish except a few.

(17. 63) He said: Be gone! For whoever of them will follow you, then surely hell is your recompense, a full recompense.

An alternative version can be found in the Book of Enoch (chapters 8–11), ascribed to the great-grandson of Noah, but more likely dating back to around 300 BC:

Moreover Azazyel taught men to make swords, knives, shields, breastplates, the fabrication of mirrors, and the workmanship of bracelets and ornaments, the use of paint, the beautifying of the eyebrows, *the use of* stones of every valuable and select kind, and all sorts of dyes, so that the world became altered.

Impiety increased; fornication multiplied; and they transgressed and corrupted all their ways. Amazarak taught all the sorcerers, and dividers of roots: Armers *taught* the solution of sorcery; Barkayal *taught* the observers of the stars, Akibeel *taught* signs, Tamiel taught astronomy, and Asaradel taught the motion of the moon. And men, being destroyed, cried out; and their voice reached to heaven.

Then Michael and Gabriel, Raphael, Suryal, and Uriel, looked down from heaven, and saw the quantity of blood which was shed on earth, and all the iniquity which was done upon it, and said one to another, *It is* the voice of their cries; The earth deprived *of her children* has cried even to the gate of heaven. And now to you, O you holy one of heaven, the souls of men complain, saying, Obtain Justice for us with the Most High. Then they said to their Lord, the King, *You are* Lord of lords, God of gods, King of kings. The throne of your glory is for ever and ever, and for ever and ever is your name sanctified and glorified. You are blessed and glorified.

You have made all things; you possess power over

all things; and all things are open and manifest before you. You behold all things, and nothing can be concealed from you. You have seen what Azazyel has done, how he has taught every species of iniquity upon earth, and has disclosed to the world all the secret things which are done in the heavens. Samyaza also has taught sorcery, to whom you have given authority over those who are associated with him. They have gone together to the daughters of men; have lain with them; have become polluted; And have discovered crimes to them.

The women likewise have brought forth giants. Thus has the whole earth been filled with blood and with iniquity. And now behold the souls of those who are dead, cry out. And complain even to the gate of heaven Their groaning ascends; nor can they escape from the unrighteousness which is committed on earth. You now all things, before they exist. You know these things, and what has been done by them; yet you do not speak to us. What on account of these things ought we to do to them?

Then the Most High, the Great and Holy One spoke, And sent Arsayalalyur to the son of Lamech, Saying, Say to him in my name, Conceal yourself. Then explain to him the consummation which is about to take place; for all the earth shall perish; the waters of a deluge shall come over the whole earth, and all things which are in it shall be destroyed. And now teach him how he may escape, and how his seed may remain in all the earth.

Again the Lord said to Raphael, Bind Azazyel hand and foot; cast him into darkness; and opening the

desert which is in Dudael, cast him in there. Throw
upon him hurled and pointed stones, covering him
with darkness; There shall he remain for ever; cover
his face, that he may not see the light. And in the great
day of judgment let him be cast into the fire.

From the Shemhamphorash section of the Goetia, or
Lesser Key of Solomon, an early *grimoire* (see p. 25), this
extract tells of one of the first lessons in demonology, the
story of how the Jewish King Solomon captured the
seventy-two demons. This translation is by two leading
occultists – S. L. MacGregor Mathers and the infamous
Aleister Crowley – from manuscripts in the British
Library:

Solomon Commanded into a Vessel of Brass, together
with their Legions. Of whom BELIAL, BILETH,
ASMODAY, and GAAP, were Chief. And it is to be
noted that Solomon did this because of their pride, for
he never declared other reason why he thus bound
them.

And when he had thus bound them up and sealed
the Vessel, he by Divine Power did chase them all into
a deep Lake or Hole in Babylon. And they of Babylon,
wondering to see such a thing, they did then go wholly
into the Lake, to break the Vessel open, expecting to
find great store of Treasure therein.

But when they had broken it open, out flew the
Chief Spirits immediately, with their Legions following them; and they were all restored to their former
places except BELIAL, who entered into a certain
Image, and thence gave answers unto those who did

offer Sacrifices unto him, and did worship the Image as their God, etc.

The temptation of Christ while he was in the desert is one of the first New Testament descriptions of the Devil. Here is the translation from the King James Bible, Matthew chapter 4 verses 1–11:

1. Then was Jesus led up of the Spirit into the wilderness to be tempted of the devil.

2. And when he had fasted forty days and forty nights, he was afterward an hungred.

3. And when the tempter came to him, he said, If thou be the Son of God, command that these stones be made bread.

4. But he answered and said, It is written, Man shall not live by bread alone, but by every word that proceedeth out of the mouth of God.

5. Then the devil taketh him up into the holy city, and setteth him on a pinnacle of the temple,

6. And saith unto him, If thou be the Son of God, cast thyself down: for it is written, He shall give his angels charge concerning thee: and in their hands they shall bear thee up, lest at any time thou dash thy foot against a stone.

7. Jesus said unto him, It is written again, Thou shalt not tempt the Lord thy God.

8. Again, the devil taketh him up into an exceeding high mountain, and sheweth him all the kingdoms of the world, and the glory of them;

9. And saith unto him, All these things will I give thee, if thou wilt fall down and worship me.

10. Then saith Jesus unto him, Get thee hence, Satan: for it is written, Thou shalt worship the Lord thy God, and him only shalt thou serve.

11. Then the devil leaveth him, and, behold, angels came and ministered unto him.

Early Witchcraft

The *Canon Episcopi* was the most important document on witchcraft in the tenth century, and became the official doctrine of the Catholic Church:

> Those who are held captive by the Devil who, leaving their creator, seek the aid of the Devil. And so Holy Church must be cleansed of this pest. It is also not to be omitted that some unconstrained women, perverted by Satan, seduced by illusions and phantasms of demons, believe and openly profess that, in the dead of night, they ride upon certain beasts with the pagan goddess Diana, with a countless horde of women, and in the silence of the dead of the night to fly over vast tracts of country, and to obey her commands as their mistress, and to be summoned to her service on other nights.
>
> But it were well if they alone perished in their infidelity and did not draw so many others into the pit of their faithlessness. For an innumerable multitude, deceived by this false opinion, believe this to be true and, so believing, wander from the right faith and relapse into pagan errors when they think that there is any divinity or power except the one God.
>
> Wherefore the priests throughout their churches should preach with all insistence to the people that they may know this to be in every way false, and that

such phantasms are sent by the devil who deludes them in dreams. Thus Satan himself, who transforms himself into an angel of light, when he has captured the mind of a miserable woman and has subjected her to himself by infidelity and incredulity, immediately changes himself into the likeness of different personages and deluding the mind which he holds captive and exhibiting things, both joyful and sorrowful, and persons, both known and unknown, and leads her faithless mind through devious ways.

The trial of Lady Alice Kyteler in Ireland in 1324 (see p. 42, 92) was the first extant record of a witchcraft trial. This extract is supposedly from a contemporary account:

The Bishop of Ossory at this period was Richard de Ledrede, a Franciscan friar, and an Englishman by birth. He soon learnt that things were not as they should be, for when making a visitation of his diocese early in 1324 he found by an Inquisition, in which were five knights and numerous nobles, that there was in the city a band of heretical sorcerers, at the head of whom was Dame Alice. The following charges were laid against them.

1. They had denied the faith of Christ absolutely for a year or a month, according as the object they desired to gain through sorcery was of greater or less importance. During all that period they believed in none of the doctrines of the Church; they did not adore the Body of Christ, nor enter a sacred building to hear mass, nor make use of consecrated bread or holy water.

2. They offered in sacrifice to demons living animals, which they dismembered, and then distributed at cross-roads to a certain evil spirit of low rank, named the Son of Art.

3. They sought by their sorcery advice and responses from demons.

4. In their nightly meetings they blasphemously imitated the power of the Church by fulminating sentence of excommunication, with lighted candles, even against their own husbands, from the sole of their foot to the crown of their head, naming each part expressly, and then concluded by extinguishing the candles and by crying *Fi! Fi! Fi! Amen.*

In order to arouse feelings of love or hatred, or to inflict death or disease on the bodies of the faithful, they made use of powders, unguents, ointments, and candles of fat, which were compounded as follows. They took the entrails of cocks sacrificed to demons, certain horrible worms, various unspecified herbs, dead men's nails, the hair, brains, and shreds of the cerements of boys who were buried unbaptized, with other abominations, all of which they cooked, with various incantations, over a fire of oak-logs in a vessel made out of the skull of a decapitated thief.

The children of Dame Alice's four husbands accused her before the Bishop of having killed their fathers by sorcery, and of having brought on them such stolidity of their senses that they bequeathed all their wealth to her and her favourite son, William Outlaw, to the impoverishment of the other children. They also stated that her present husband, Sir John le Poer, had been reduced to such a condition by sorcery and the use of powders that he had become terribly emaciated, his nails had dropped off, and there was no hair left on his body [. . .]

The said dame had a certain demon, an incubus, named Son of Art, or Robin son of Art, who had carnal knowledge of her, and from whom she admitted that she had received all her wealth. This incubus made its appearance under various forms, sometimes as a cat, or as a hairy black dog, or in the likeness of a negro (Æthiops), accompanied by two others who were larger and taller than he, and of whom one carried an iron rod.

The Book of the Sacred Magic of Abramelin the Mage, published in 1458, contains a fascinating account of night riding with a witch:

At LINTZ I worked with a young woman, who one evening invited me to go with her, assuring me that without any risk she would conduct me to a place where I greatly desired to find myself. I allowed myself to be persuaded by her promises. She then gave unto me an unguent, with which I rubbed the principal pulses of my feet and hands; the which she did also; and at first it appeared to me that I was flying in the air in the place which I wished, and which I had in no way mentioned to her ... I felt as if I were just awakening from a profound sleep, and I had great pain in my head and deep melancholy. I turned round and saw that she was seated at my side.

She began to recount to me what she had seen, but that which I had seen was entirely different. I was, however, much astonished, because it appeared to me as if I had been really and corporeally in the place, and there in reality to have seen that which had happened. However, I asked her one day to go alone to that same place, and to bring me back news of a friend whom I knew for certain was distant 200 leagues.

She promised to do so in the space of an hour. She rubbed herself with the same unguent, and I was very expectant to see her fly away; but she fell to the ground and remained there about three hours as if she were dead, so that I began to think that she really was dead. At last she began to stir like a person who is waking, then she rose to an upright position, and with much pleasure began to give me the account of her expedition, saying that she had been in the place where my friend was, and all that he was doing; the which was entirely contrary to his profession. Whence I concluded that what she had just told me was a simple dream, and that this unguent was a causer of a phantastic sleep; whereon she confessed to me that this unguent had been given to her by the Devil.

The *Formicarius* by Johannes Nider, published in 1476, outlines some of the first methods of persecution against witches in Europe:

The ceremony, he said, of my seduction was as follows: First, on a Sunday, before the holy water is consecrated, the future disciple with his masters must go into the church, and there in their presence must renounce Christ and his faith, baptism, and the church universal. Then he must do homage to the magisterulus, that is, to the little master (for so, and not otherwise, they call the Devil). Afterward he drinks from the aforesaid flask: and, this done, he forthwith feels himself to conceive and hold within himself an image of our art and the chief rites of this sect. After this fashion was I seduced; and my wife also, whom I believe of so great pertinacity that she will endure the flames rather than confess the least whit of the truth; but, alas, we are both guilty.

What the young man had said was found in all respects the truth. For, after confession, the young man was seen to die in great contrition. His wife, however, though convicted by the testimony of witnesses, would not confess the truth even under the torture or in death; but when the fire was prepared for her by the executioner, uttered in most evil words a curse upon him, and so was burned.

The Hammer of the Witches: *Malleus Maleficarum*

Written in 1486 by the Catholic Inquisitor Heinrich Kramer and Jacob Sprenger, the *Maleficarum* is the most famous early modern handbook for witch hunters and was written to set out in staggering detail the ways and weaknesses of the possessed. This extract reveals how the Devil tempts the Innocent through witches:

There are three methods above all by which devils, through the agency of witches, subvert the innocent, and by which that perfidy is continually being increased. And the first is through weariness, through inflicting grievous losses in their temporal possessions. For, as S. Gregory says: The devil often tempts us to give way from very weariness. And it is to be understood that it is within the power of a man to resist such temptation ... Devils, therefore, by means of witches, so afflict their innocent neighbours with temporal losses, that they are to beg the suffrages of witches, and at length to submit themselves to their counsels; as many experiences have taught us.

We know a stranger in the diocese of Augsburg, who before he was forty-four years old lost all his horses in succession through witchcraft. His wife, being afflicted with weariness by reason of this, consulted with witches, and after following their counsels, unwholesome as they were, all the horses which he bought after that (for he was a carrier) were preserved from witchcraft ...

Here it is to be noted that, as has already been hinted, this iniquity has small and scant beginnings, as that of the time of the elevation of the Body of Christ they spit on the ground, or shut their eyes, or mutter some vain words. We know a woman who yet lives, protected by the secular law, who, when the priest at the celebration of the Mass blesses the people, saying, *Dominus uobiscum*, always adds to herself these words in the vulgar tongue 'Kehr mir die Zung im Arss umb.' Or they even say some such thing at confession after they have received absolution, or do not confess everything, especially mortal sins, and so by slow degrees are led to a total abnegation of the Faith, and to the abominable profession of sacrilege.

This, or something like it, is the method which witches use towards honest matrons who are little given to carnal vices but concerned for worldly profit. But towards young girls, more given to bodily lusts and pleasures, they observe a different method, working through their carnal desires and the pleasures of the flesh.

Here it is to be noted that the devil is more eager and keen to tempt the good than the wicked, although in actual practice he tempts the wicked more than the good, because more aptitude for being tempted is found in the wicked than in the good. Therefore the devil tries all the harder to seduce all the more saintly virgins and girls; and there is reason in this, besides many examples of it . . .

There is also a third method of temptation through the way of sadness and poverty. For when girls have been corrupted, and have been scorned by their lovers after they have immodestly copulated with them in the hope and promise of marriage with them, and have found themselves disappointed in all their hopes and everywhere despised, they turn to the help and protection of devils; either for the sake of vengeance by bewitching those lovers or the wives they have married, or for the sake of giving themselves up to every sort of lechery. Alas! experience tells us that there is no number to such girls, and consequently the witches that spring from this class are innumerable.

From this it is clear that witches use various methods to increase their numbers. For the above-mentioned woman, because she had been supplanted by the Count's wife, case that spell upon the Count with the help of another witches; and this is how one witchcraft brings innumerable others in its train.

The *Maleficarum* also included advice on how to combat witchcraft and prosecute the accused. In this section it promotes the use of tests to identify the guilty:

The Judge should act as follows in the continuation of
the torture. First he should bear in mind that, just as
the same medicine is not applicable to all the members,
but there are various and distinct salves for each
several member, so not all heretics or those accused of
heresy are to be subjected to the same method of
questioning, examination and torture as to the charges
laid against them; but various and different means are
to be employed according to their various natures and
persons. Now a surgeon cuts off rotten limbs; and
mangy sheep are isolated from the healthy; but a
prudent Judge will not consider it safe to bind himself
down to one invariable rule in his method of dealing
with a prisoner who is endowed with a witch's power
of taciturnity, and whose silence he is unable to
overcome. For if the sons of darkness were to become
accustomed to one general rule they would provide
means of evading it as a well-known snare set for their
destruction . . .

If he wishes to find out whether she is endowed
with a witch's power of preserving silence, let him take
note whether she is able to shed tears when standing
in his presence, or when being tortured . . . if she be a
witch she will not be able to weep: although she will
assume a tearful aspect and smear her cheeks and eyes
with spittle to make it appear that she is weeping;
wherefore she must be closely watched by the
attendants . . . And as for the reason for a witch's
inability to weep, it can be said that the grace of tears
is one of the chief gifts allowed to the penitent.

A second precaution is to be observed, not only at
this point but during the whole process, by the Judge

and all his assessors; namely, that they must not allow themselves to be touched physically by the witch, especially in any contact of their bare arms or hands; but they must always carry about them some salt consecrated on Palm Sunday and some Blessed Herbs. For these can be enclosed together in Blessed Wax and worn round the neck . . . But let it not be thought that physical contact of the joints or limbs is the only thing to be guarded against; for sometimes, with God's permission, they are able with the help of the devil to bewitch the Judge by the mere sound of the words which they utter, especially at the time when they are exposed to torture.

And we know from experience that some witches, when detained in prison, have importunately begged their gaolers to grant them this one thing, that they should be allowed to look at the Judge before he looks at them; and by so getting the first sight of the Judge they have been able so to alter the minds of the Judge or his assessors that they have lost all their anger against them and have not presumed to molest them in any way, but have allowed them to go free. He who knows and has experienced it gives this true testimony; and would that they were not able to effect such things!

The third precaution to be observed in this tenth action is that the hair should be shaved from every part of her body. The reason for this is the same as that for stripping her of her clothes, which we have already mentioned; for in order to preserve their power of silence they are in the habit of hiding some superstitious object in their clothes or in their hair, or even in the most secret parts of their bodies which must not be named.

But it may be objected that the devil might, without the use of such charms, so harden the heart of a witch that she is unable to confess her crimes; just as it is often found in the case of other criminals, no matter how great the tortures to which they are exposed, or how much they are convicted by the evidence of the facts and of witnesses . . .

This can be made clear from the example of a certain witch in the town of Hagenau. She used to obtain this gift of silence in the following manner: she killed a newly-born first-born male child who had not been baptized, and having roasted it in an oven together with other matters which it is not expedient to mention, ground it to powder and ashes; and if any witch or criminal carried about him some of this substance he would in no way be able to confess his crimes . . .

Yet the *Maleficarum* went beyond the use of tests, and endorsed torture in order to gain a conviction:

A Judge, who is responsible for the safety of the community, may lawfully allow a smaller evil that a greater may be avoided . . . since less hurt is caused to the hands by the red-hot iron than is the loss of life in a duel, if a duel is permitted where such things are customary, much more should the trial by red-hot iron be allowed . . . I answer that such tests or trials are unlawful for two reasons. First, because their purpose is to judge of hidden matters of which it belongs only to God to judge. Secondly, because there is no Divine authority for such trials, nor are they anywhere sanctioned in the writings of the Holy Fathers.

Extracts from the papal bull of Innocent VIII of 9 December 1484, that gave the Catholic Church's support to the persecution of witchcraft:

It has indeed lately come to Our ears, not without afflicting Us with bitter sorrow, that in some parts of Northern Germany, as well as in the provinces, townships, territories, districts, and dioceses of Mainz, Cologne, Tréves, Salzburg, and Bremen, many persons of both sexes, unmindful of their own salvation and straying from the Catholic Faith, have abandoned themselves to devils, incubi and succubi, and by their incantations, spells, conjurations, and other accursed charms and crafts, enormities and horrid offences, have slain infants yet in the mother's womb, as also the offspring of cattle, have blasted the produce of the earth, the grapes of the vine, the fruits of the trees, nay, men and women, beasts of burthen, herd-beasts, as well as animals of other kinds, vineyards, orchards, meadows, pasture-land, corn, wheat, and all other cereals; these wretches furthermore afflict and torment men and women, beasts of burthen, herd-beasts, as well as animals of other kinds, with terrible and piteous pains and sore diseases, both internal and external; they hinder men from performing the sexual act and women from conceiving, whence husbands cannot know their wives nor wives receive their husbands; over and above this, they blasphemously renounce that Faith which is theirs by the Sacrament of Baptism, and at the instigation of the Enemy of Mankind they do not shrink from committing and perpetrating the foulest abominations and filthiest excesses to the deadly peril of their own souls, whereby they outrage the Divine Majesty and are a cause of scandal and danger to very many ...

We decree and enjoin that the aforesaid Inquisitors be empowered to proceed to the just correction, imprisonment, and punishment of any persons, without let or hindrance, in every way as if the provinces, townships, dioceses, districts, territories, yea, even the persons and their crimes in this kind were named and particularly designated in Our letters. Moreover, for greater surety We extend these letters deputing this authority to cover all the aforesaid provinces, townships, dioceses, districts, territories, persons, and crimes newly rehearsed, and We grant permission to the aforesaid Inquisitors ... to proceed, according to the regulations of the Inquisition, against any persons of whatsoever rank and high estate, correcting, mulcting, imprisoning, punishing, as their crimes merit, those whom they have found guilty, the penalty being adapted to the offence.

The Witch Craze

Accounts of witch tests sourced from Paul Carus's 1900 book *The History of the Devil* show the extent of the horror in many of the cases. The first is a summary of a trial in 1631:

The hangman binds the woman, who was pregnant, and places her on the rack. Then he racked her till her heart would fain break, but had no compassion. When she did not confess, the torture was repeated, the hangman tied her hands, cut off her hair, poured brandy over her head and burned it. He placed sulphur in her armpits and burned it. Her hands were tied behind her, and she was hauled up to the ceiling and suddenly dropped down. This hauling up and dropping down was repeated for some hours, until the hangman and his helpers went to dinner.

When they returned, the master-hangman tied her feet and hands upon her back; brandy was poured on her back and burned. Then heavy weights were placed on her back and she was pulled up. After this she was again stretched on the rack. A spiked board is placed on her back, and she is again hauled up to the ceiling. The master again ties her feet and hangs on them a block of fifty pounds, which makes her think that her heart will burst. This proved insufficient; therefore the master unties her feet and fixes her legs in a vise, tightening the jaws until the blood oozes out at the toes.

Nor was this sufficient; therefore she was stretched and pinched again in various ways. Now the hangman of Dreissigacker began the third grade of torture. When he placed her on the bench and put the I shirt on her, he said: 'I do not take you for one, two, three, not for eight days, nor for a few weeks, but for half a year or a year, for your whole life, until you confess: and if you will not confess, I shall torture you to death, and you shall be burned after all.' The hangman's son-in-law hauled her up to the ceiling by her hands. The hangman of Dreissigacker whipped her with a horsewhip. She was placed in a vise where she remained for six hours. After that she was again mercilessly horsewhipped. This was all that was done on the first day.

Another account shows how superstition and jealousy often turned into accusations of witchcraft:

There was a farmer by the name of Veit, living in a village of Southern Bohemia. He was famous for his wit and unusual humor. At the same time he was physically strong, and whenever there was a quarrel at the inn he came off victor. The rumor spread that he was inviolable, as sometimes hunters are supposed to be bullet-proof, and Veit never denied it. By and by he was regarded as a wizard, and as his cattle prospered best and his fields yielded the richest crops, he was soon supposed to be in league with the Evil One.

Now it happened that the village was troubled with mice, and Veit was suspected of having caused the plague. When questioned about it, he granted in a moment of humor that he had sent the mice but would soon drive them away again, and he promised to prove at the next church-fair that he could actually make mice. When the day appointed came, the inn was overcrowded, and farmer Veit appeared with a big bag under his arm, into which he requested the company to throw twenty pebbles. They did so without noticing that the bag was double. And while one part was empty the other contained twenty mice. When the pebbles were put in the bag, Veit murmured a magic formula and let the mice loose in the presence of his frightened audience.

This performance, however, had unexpected and tragic results. The people were convinced that it was the work of hell, and Veit escaped with difficulty from the inn. Veit was arrested the next night and delivered to the criminal court. A mole on his body was thought to be a stigma of the Devil, and all the witnesses agreed that he was a genuine wizard.

His case was thoroughly investigated, and even the University of Prague was consulted; the verdict signed by the Rector Magnificus with his own hand was against him, and Veit, who stoutly maintained his innocence, had to endure all the tortures of the inquisition. At last he was burned alive and the ashes of his body were thrown to the winds. We read in the records of the law-suit that Veit mounted the stake 'without showing repentance or doing penance.' And when chains were put on his neck, around his body, and around his feet, he cried with a loud voice, 'My God, I die innocently.' Judges, professors, physicians, and theologians agreed unanimously in the conviction of this innocent man.

Witchcraft in Britain
Henry VIII's 1542 statue against witchcraft was the first law passed by parliament that outlined the persecution of magic, and was swiftly repealed by Edward VI:

After the first day of May next comyng, use, devise, practise or exercise, or cause to be devysed, practised or exercised, any Invovacons or cojuracons of Sprites witchecraftes enchauntementes or sorceries to the intent to fynde money or treasure or to waste,

consume or destroy any person in his bodie membres,
or to pvoke [provoke] any person to unlawfull love, or
for any other unlawfull intente or purpose ... or for
dispite of Cryste, or for lucre of money, dygge up or
pull downe any Crosse or Crosses or by such
Invovacons or cojuracons of Sprites witchecraftes
enchauntementes or sorceries or any of them take
upon them to tell or declare where goodes stollen or
lost shall from the saide first day of May next comyng
shall be demyde accepted and adjuged felonye.

Reginald Scott's *The Discoverie of Witchcraft*, published
in 1584, was one of the first attacks on the superstitious
belief in England:

It is strange, that we should suppose, that such persons
can work such feats: and it is more strange, that we
will imagine that to be possible to be done by a witch,
which to nature and sense is impossible; specially
when our neighbours life depended upon our credulity therein; and when we may see the defect of ability,
which always is an impediment both to the act, and
also to the presumption thereof. And because there is
nothing possible in law, that in nature is impossible;
therefore the judge doth not attend or regard what the
accused man said; or yet would do: but what is proved
to have been committed, and naturally fell in man's
power and will to do.

For the law said, that to will a thing impossible, is a
sign of a mad man, or of a fool, upon whom no
sentence or judgement taken hold. Furthermore, what
jury will condemn, or what judge will give sentence or

judgement against one for killing a man at Berwick; when they themselves, and many other saw that man at London, that very day, wherein the murder was committed; yea though the party confess himself guilty therein, and twenty witnesses depose the same? But in this case also I say the judge is not to weigh their testimony, which is weakened by law; and the judge's authority is to supply the imperfection of the case, and to maintain the right and equity of the same.

Seeing therefore that some other things might naturally be the occasion and cause of such calamities as witches are supposed to bring; let not us that profess the Gospel and knowledge of Christ, be bewitched to believe that they do such things, as are in nature impossible, and in sense and reason incredible. If they say it is done through the devil's help, who can work miracles; why do not thieves bring their business to pass miraculously, with whom the devil is as conversant as with the other? Such mischiefs as are imputed to witches, happen where no witches are; yea and continue when witches are hanged and burnt: why then should we attribute such effect to that cause, which being taken away, happened nevertheless?

The Pendle Hill witch trial was the first prosecution following James I's 1604 new law. In the confession of Old Demdike, she recounts how she was first seduced by 'Tibb':

... about twenty years past, as she was coming homeward from begging, there met her near unto a stonepit in Gouldshey, in the said forest of Pendle, a spirit or devil in the shape of a boy, the one half of his coat black, and the other brown, who bade this [defendant] stay, saying to her, that if she would give him her soul, she should have any thing that she would request. Whereupon the [defendant] demanded his name? And the spirit answered, his name was tibb: and so the [defendant] in hope of such gain as was promised by the said devil or tibb, was contented to give her soul to the said spirit: and for the space of five or six years next after, the said spirit or devil appeared at sundry times unto her the [defendant] about day-light gate, always bidding her stay, and asking her what she would have or do. To whom the [defendant] replied, nay nothing: for she said, she wanted nothing yet.

And so about the end of the said six years, upon a sabbath day in the morning, the [defendant] having a little child upon her knee, and she being in a slumber, the said spirit appeared unto her in the likeness of a brown dog, forcing himself to her knee, to get blood under her left arm: and she being without any apparel saving her smock, the said devil did get blood under her left arm. And the [defendant] awaking, said, Jesus save my child; but had no power, nor could not say, Jesus save her self: whereupon the brown dog vanished out of sight: after which, the [defendant] was almost stark mad for the space of eight weeks.

Later in her confession, Demdike tells how she was taught how to kill a man:

And further the [defendant] confessed, and said, that the speediest way to take a man's life away by witchcraft, is to make a picture of clay, like unto the shape of the person whom they mean to kill, & dry it thoroughly: and when they would have them to be ill in any one place more then another; then take a thorn or pin, and prick it in that part of the picture you would so have to be ill: and when you would have any part of the body to consume away, then take that part of the picture, and burn it. And when they would have the whole body to consume away, then take the remnant of the said picture, and burn it: and so thereupon by that means, the body shall die.

During the civil wars of 1642–8, Matthew Hopkins gained the name of Witchfinder General, as recounted in his 1647 book *The Discoverie of Witches*. Here is one account of a trial in Manningtree, Essex:

In *March* 1644 he had [judged] some seven or eight of that horrible sect of Witches living in the Town where he lived, a Town in Essex called *Maningtree*, with diverse other adjacent Witches of other towns, who every six weeks in the night (being always on the Friday night) had their meeting close by his house and had their several solemn sacrifices there offered to the *Devil*, one of which this discoverer heard speaking to her Imps one night, and bid them go to another Witch, who was thereupon apprehended, and searched, by women who had for many years known the Devil's marks, and found to have three teats about her, which honest women have not.

Upon command from the *Justice* they were to keep her from sleep two or three nights, expecting in that time to see her *familiars*, which the fourth night she called in by their several names, and told them what shapes, a quarter of an hour before they came in, there being ten of us in the room, the first she called was

1. *Holt*, who came in like a white kitling.

2. *Jarmara*, who came in like a fat Spaniel without any legs at all, she said she kept him fat, for she clapped her hand on her belly and said he sucked good blood from her body.

3. *Vinegar Tom*, who was like a long-legg'd Greyhound, with an head like an Ox, with a long tail and broad eyes, who when this discoverer spoke to, and bade him go to the place provided for him and his Angels, immediately transformed himself into the shape of a child of four years old without a head, and gave half a dozen turns about the house, and vanished at the door.

4. *Sack and Sugar*, like a black Rabbit.

5. *Newes*, like a Polecat.

All these vanished away in a little time. Immediately after this Witch confessed several other Witches, from whom she had her *Imps*, and named to divers women where their marks were, the number of their *Marks*, and *Imps*, and *Imps* names, as *Elemanzer*, *Pyewacket*, *Peckin the Crown*, *Grizzel*, *Greedigut*, &c. which no mortal could invent; and upon their searches the same Marks were found, the same number, and in the same place, and the like confessions from them of the same Imps, (though they knew not that we were told before) and so peached one another thereabouts that joined together in the like damnable practise that in our Hundred in *Essex* 29 were condemned at once.

Witchcraft in America

Even before the witch trial of Salem, there was wide-spread belief in witches. Cotton Mather's 1689 *Memorable Providences* tells the story of recent possessions in Boston and warns about any argument against the phenomenon:

> Go tell Mankind, that there are Devils and Witches; and that tho those night-birds least appear where the Day-light of the Gospel comes, yet New-Engl. has had Exemples of their Existence and Operation; and that no only the Wigwams of Indians, where the pagan Powaws often raise their masters, in the shapes of Bears and Snakes and Fires, but the House of Christians, where our God has had his constant Worship, have undergone the Annoyance of Evil spirits . . .
>
> I do now likewise publish the History, While the thing is yet fresh and New; and I challenge all men to detect so much as one designed Falshood, yea, or so much as one important Mistake, from the Egg to the Apple of it. I have Writ as plainly as becomes an Historian, as truly as becomes a Christian, tho perhaps not so profitably as became a Divine. But I am resolv'd after this, never to use but just one grain of patience with any man that shall go to impose upon me a Denial of Devils, or of Witches. I shall count that man Ignorant who shall suspect, but I shall count him down-right Impudent if he Assert the Non-Existence of things which we have had such palpable convictions of.

Deodat Lawson was the minister at Salem from 1684–8, before the trials began. He published his 'Brief and True

Narrative' in 1692, which begins with his return to the community, where he first encountered the 'afflicted women':

On the Nineteenth day of March last I went to Salem Village, and lodged at Nathaniel Ingersols near to the Minister Mr. P's (Parris). house, and presently after I came into my Lodging Capt. Walcuts Daughter Mary came to Lieut. Ingersols and spoke to me, but, suddenly after as she stood by the door, was bitten, so that she cried out of her Wrist, and looking on it with a Candle, we saw apparently the marks of Teeth both upper and lower set, on each side of her wrist.

In the beginning of the Evening, I went to give Mr. P. (Parris) a visit. When I was there, his Kinswoman, Abigail Williams, (about 12 years of age,) had a grievous fit; she was at first hurried with Violence to and fro in the room, (though Mrs. Ingersol endeavoured to hold her,) sometimes making as if she would fly, stretching up her arms as high as she could, and crying 'Whish, Whish, Whish!' several times; Presently after she said there was Goodw. Nurse. and said, 'Do you not see her? Why there she stands!' And the said Goodw. N. offered her The Book, but she was resolved she would not take it, saying Often, 'I won't, I won't, I won't, take it, I do not know what Book it is: I am sure it is none of Gods Book, it is the Devil's Book, for ought I know.' After that, she run to the Fire, and begun to throw Fire Brands, about the house; and run against the Back, as if she would run up Chimney and, as they said, she had attempted to go into the Fire in other Fits.

This is the transcript of Sarah Osbourne's examination on 1 March 1693:

Salem Village March the 1'st 1691/2

Sarah Osburne the wife of Alexander Osburne of Salem Village. brought before us by Joseph Herrick Constable in Salem, to Answer Joseph Hutcheson & Thomas Putnam &c yeomen in s'd Salem Village Complainants on behalf of their Majesty's against s'd Sarah Osburne, for Suspicion of Witchcraft by her Committed, and thereby much Injury done to the Bodiess of Elizabeth Parris, Abigail Williams Anna Putnam and Elizabeth Hubert all of Salem Village aforesaid, according to their Complaint, according to a Warrant, Dated Salem febu'y 29'th 1691/2.

Sarah Osburne upon Examination denied the matter of fact (viz) that she ever understood or used any Witchcraft, or hurt any of the above s'd children.

The children above named being all personally present accused her face to face which being don, they were all hurt, afflicted and tortured very much: which being over and they out of their fits they said that said Sarah Osburne did then Come to them and hurt them, Sarah Osburn being then kept at a distance personally from them. S. Osburne was asked why she then hurt them, she denied it: it being Asked of her how she could so pinch and hurt them and yet she be at that distance personally from them she answered she did not then hurt them nor never did she was Asked who then did it, or who she employed to do it, she Answered she did not know that the devil goes about in her likeness to do any hurt. Sarah Osburn

being told that Sarah Good one of her Companions
had upon.

Despite her protestations of innocence, Sarah Good, the
co-defendant alongside Sarah Osbourne, was sentenced
to death alongside the others accused:

Whereas Sarah Good Wife of William Good of Salem
Village, Rebecka Nurse wife of Francis Nurse of Salem
Villiage, Susanna Martin of Amesbury, Widow Eliza-
beth How wife of James How of Ipswich, Sarah Wild
Wife of John Wild of Topsfield, all of the County of
Essex in their Maj'ts Province of the Massachusetts
Bay in New England. At a court held by adjournment
for Our Sovereign Lord & Lady King William &
Queen Mary for the said County of Essex at Salem in
the s'd County on the 29th day of June were Severally
arraigned on several Indictments for the horrible
Crime of Witchcraft by them practised and committed
on several persons and pleading not guilty did for their
trial put themselves on God & their country whereupon they were each of them found and brought in
Guilty by the Jury that passed. On them according to
their respective Indictments and Sentence of death did
then pass upon them as the Law directs Execution
whereof yet remains to be done:

Those are Therefore in their Majesties name William
& Mary now King & Queen over England &ca: to will
& Command you that upon Tuesday next being the
19th day of [torn] Instant July between the hours of
Eight & the forenoon the same day you Elizabeth
How & Sarah Wild From their Majest's Goal in Salem

afores'd to the place of Execution & there Cause them & Every of them to be hanged by the Neck until they be dead and of the doings herein make return to the Clerke of the said Court & this precept and hereof you are not to fail at your peril and this Shall be your Sufficient Warrant.

Given under my hand & seal at Boston the 12'th day of July in the fourth year of the Reign of our Soveraigne Lord & Lady Wm & Mary King and Queen &ca:

*Wm Stoughton

The father of Cotton Mather, Increase Mather, who went to Salem, was concerned that the trials lacked legal standing. His interventions in *Cases of Conscience Concerning Evil Spirits* (1693) supported the judges but questioned their methods:

That there are Devils and Witches, the Scripture asserts, and experience confirms, That they are common enemies of Mankind, and set upon mischief, is not to be doubted: That the Devil can (by Divine Permission) and often doth vex men in Body and Estate, without the Instrumentality of Witches, is undeniable: That he often hath, and delights to have the concurrence of Witches, and their consent in harming men, is consonant to his native Malice to Man, and too lamentably exemplified . . .

We judge that in the prosecution of these, and all such Witchcrafts, there is need of a very critical and exquisite Caution, lest by too much Credulity for things received only upon the Devil's Authority, there be a Door opened for a long Train of miserable Consequences, and Satan get an advantage over us, for we should not be ignorant of his Devices ...

As in Complaints upon Witchcrafts, there may be Matters of Enquiry, which do not amount unto Matters of Presumption, and there may be Matters of Presumption which yet may not be reckoned Matters of Conviction; so 'tis necessary that all Proceedings thereabout be managed with an exceeding tenderness towards those that may be complained of; especially if they have been Persons formerly of an unblemished Reputation.

Witchcraft and Reason

Joseph Addison was one of the editors of the leading enlightenment periodical, the *Spectator*. In 1711, he made his opinions on witchcraft clear:

I think a Person who is thus terrified with the Imagination of Ghosts and Spectres much more reasonable, than one who contrary to the Reports of all Historians sacred and profane, ancient and modern, and to the Traditions of all Nations, thinks the Appearance of Spirits fabulous and groundless ... When I consider the Question, Whether there are such Persons in the World as those we call Witches? My mind is divided between the two opposite Opinions; or rather (to speak my Thoughts freely) I believe in general that there is, and has been such a thing as Witchcraft; but at the same time can give no Credit to any Particular Instance of it.

The French philosopher Voltaire was highly critical of any argument for witchcraft:

The witches have stopped to exist when we have stopped to burn them.

The French *Encyclopédie* has no entry on witchcraft but its short precis on the existence of the incubus is a strong indication of the feelings of Enlightenment philosophers:

It is more reasonable to think that all that is known of *incubi*, even including the statements of witches, is the result of an ardent imagination and a fiery temperament. From women abandoned to the deprivations of their heart, aflame with impure desires, having dreams and hallucinations and believing that they had relations with demons, there is nothing there so stunning in imagining being transported through the air on a broom stick, dancing, feasting, adoring the 'goat,' and having relations with him or with his henchmen.

All these things, however, happen beyond the plane of the senses, rather they are the effects of a vivid imagination; it requires only the least bit more effort to suppose that *incubi* exist.

The Romantic novelist Sir Walter Scott wrote *Letters on Demonology and Witchcraft* in 1831, with the aim of entertaining and educating about the forgotten, and irrational, history of witchcraft:

It is accordingly remarkable, in different countries, how often at some particular period of their history there occurred an epidemic of terror of witches, which, as fear is always cruel and credulous, glutted the public with seas of innocent blood; and how uniformly men loathed the gore after having swallowed it, and by a reaction natural to the human mind desired, in prudence, to take away or restrict those laws which had been the source of carnage, in order that their posterity might neither have the will nor the mean to enter into similar excesses . . .

But in the meanwhile, as the accusation of witchcraft thus afforded to tyranny or policy the ready means of assailing persons whom it might not have been possible to convict of any other crime, the aspersion itself was gradually considered with increase of terror as spreading wider and becoming more contagious.

The Search for Real Witches
The fairy tales of the Grimm Brothers are full of witches. Here is one example from the story of Hansel and Gretel:

The old woman had only pretended to be so kind; she was in reality a wicked witch, who lay in wait for children, and had only built the little house of bread in order to entice them there. When a child fell into her power, she killed it, cooked and ate it, and that was a feast day with her. Witches have red eyes, and cannot see far, but they have a keen scent like the beasts, and are aware when human beings draw near. When Hansel and Gretel came into her neighbourhood, she laughed with malice, and said mockingly: 'I have them, they shall not escape me again!'

Early in the morning before the children were awake, she was already up, and when she saw both of them sleeping and looking so pretty, with their plump and rosy cheeks she muttered to herself: 'That will be a dainty mouthful!' Then she seized Hansel with her shriveled hand, carried him into a little stable, and locked him in behind a grated door. Scream as he might, it would not help him. Then she went to Gretel, shook her till she awoke, and cried: 'Get up, lazy thing, fetch some water, and cook something good for your brother, he is in the stable outside, and is to be made fat. When he is fat, I will eat him.' Gretel began to weep bitterly, but it was all in vain, for she was forced to do what the wicked witch commanded.

Jules Michelet sought to develop the idea of the witch as a social rebel, in opposition to the hierarchy of the Middle Ages, in *La Sorcière*, 1862:

The only physician of the people for a thousand years was the Witch. The emperors, kings, popes, and richer barons had indeed their doctors of Salerno, their Moors and Jews; but the bulk of people in every state, the world as it might well be called, consulted none but the *Saga*, or wise-woman. When she could not cure them, she was insulted, was called a Witch. But generally, from a respect not unmixed with fear, she was called good lady or fair lady (*belle dame – bella donna*), the very name we give to the fairies ... At what date, then, did the Witch first appear? I say unfalteringly, 'In the age of despair:' of that deep despair which the gentry of the Church engendered.

Unfalteringly do I say, 'The Witch is a crime of their own achieving'.

The neo-pagan fashion for witchcraft is exemplified by Leland's *Vangelo* or *Aradia, Gospel of the Witches*, 1899. Here are the opening pages:

This is the Gospel of the Witches:
Diana greatly loved her brother Lucifer, the god of the Sun and of the Moon, the god of Light who was so proud of his beauty, and who for his pride was driven from Paradise.

Diana had by, her brother a daughter, to whom they gave the name of Aradia [*i.e.* Herodias].

In those days there were on earth many rich and many poor.

The rich made slaves of all the poor.

In those days were many slaves who were cruelly treated; in every palace tortures, in every castle prisoners.

Many slaves escaped. They fled to the country; thus they became thieves and evil folk. Instead of sleeping by night, they plotted escape and robbed their masters, and then slew them. So they dwelt in the mountains and forests as robbers and assassins, all to avoid slavery.

Diana said one day to her daughter Aradia:

'Tis true indeed that thou a spirit art,
But thou wert born but to become again
A mortal; thou must go to earth below
To be a teacher unto women and men

Who fain would study witchcraft in thy school

Yet like Cain's daughter thou shalt never be,
Nor like the race who have become at last
Wicked and infamous from suffering,
As are the Jews and wandering Zingari,
Who are all thieves and knaves; like unto them
Ye shall not be . . .

And thou shalt be the first of witches known;
And thou shalt be the first of all I' the world;
And thou shalt teach the art of poisoning,
Of poisoning those who are great lords of all;
Yea, thou shalt make them die in their palaces;
And thou shalt bind the oppressor's soul (with power);
And when ye find a peasant who is rich,
Then ye shall teach the witch, your pupil, how
To ruin all his crops with tempests dire,
With lightning and with thunder (terrible),
And the hail and wind . . .

FURTHER READING

Agrippa, Henry Cornelius. *Three Books of Occult Philosophy* (1531), Woodbury, Minnesota: Llewellyn Publications, 1997

Charles, R.H. (trans.). *The Book of Enoch*, London: SPCK, 1994

Clark, Stuart. *Thinking With Demons: The Idea of Witchcraft in Early Modern Europe*, Oxford: Oxford University Press, 1997

Cohn, Norman. *Europe's Inner Demons: An Enquiry Inspired by the Great Witch-Hunt*, New York: New American Library, 1975

Ewen, C. L'Estrange. *Witch Hunting and Witch Trials* (1929), London: Muller, 1971

Gaskill, Malcolm. *Witchcraft: A Very Short Introduction*, Oxford: Oxford University Press, 2010

Gaskill, Malcolm. *Witchfinders: A Seventeenth-Century English Tragedy*, London: John Murray, 2006

Ginzburg, Carlo. *The Night Battles: Witchcraft and Agrarian Cults in the Sixteenth and Seventeenth Centuries* (1983), Baltimore: Johns Hopkins University Press, 1992

Ginzburg, Carlo. *Ecstasies: Deciphering the Witches' Sabbath*, New York: Pantheon Books, 1991

Guiley, Rosemary Ellen. *The Encyclopedia of Witches and Witchcraft*, Second Edition, New York: Checkmark Books, 1999

Hopkins, Matthew and Stearne, John. *The Discovery of Witches and Witchcraft: The Writings of the Witchfinders*, Brighton: Puckrel Publishing, 2007

Hutton, Ronald. *Triumph of the Moon: A History of Modern Pagan Witchcraft* (1999), Oxford: Oxford University Press, 2001

Institoris, Heinrich and Sprenger, James (trans. Montague Summers) (1486) *The Malleus Maleficarum of Heinrich Kramer and James Sprenger*, San Diego: The Book Tree, 2000

Kieckhefer, Richard. *European Witch Trials: Their Foundation in Popular and Learned Culture*, Berkeley: University of California Press, 1976

Kieckhefer, Richard. *Magic in the Middle Ages* (1989), Cambridge: Cambridge University Press, 2000

Kors, Alan C. & Peters, Edward. *Witchcraft in Europe 1100–1700: A Documentary History* (1972), Philadelphia: University of Pennsylvania Press, 1999

Leland, Charles G., *Aradia, or Gospel of the Witches* (1890), New York: Phoenix Publishing, 1990

Levack, Brian P. (ed). *The Witchcraft Sourcebook*, New York: Routledge. 2004

Levack, Brian P. *The Witch-Hunt in Early Modern Europe*, Second Edition, Harlow, Middlesex: Longman, 1995

Murray, Margaret A. *The Witch-Cult in Western Europe* (1921), New York: Barnes & Noble Books, 1996

Normand, Lawrence and Roberts, Gareth. *Witchcraft in Early Modern Scotland: James IV's Demonology and the North Berwick Witches*, Exeter: University of Exeter Press, 2000

Oldridge, Darren (ed). *The Witchcraft Reader*, Oxford: Routledge, 2002

Poole, Robert (ed). *The Lancashire Witches: Histories and Stories*, Manchester: Manchester University Press, 2002

Potts, Thomas. *The Wonderfull Discoverie of Witches in the Countie of Lancaster*, Lancaster: Carnegie Publishing, 2003

Russell, Jeffery Burton. *Lucifer: The Devil in the Middle Ages* (1984), Ithaca, NY: Cornell University Press, 1986

Russell, Jeffery Burton. *Satan: The Early Christian Tradition*, Ithaca, NY: Cornell University Press, 1981

Russell, Jeffery Burton. *Witchcraft in the Middle Ages* (1972), Ithaca, NY: Cornell University Press, 1984

Russell, Jeffery Burton. *A History of Witchcraft: Sorcerers, Heretics, Pagans* (1980), London: Thames & Hudson, 1999

Scot, Reginald. *The Discoverie of Witchcraft* (1586), New York: Dover Publications, 1980

Shah, Idries. *The Sufis* (1964), London: The Octagon Press, 1999

Thomas, Keith. *Religion and the Decline of Magic* (1971), London: Penguin Books, 1991

Thurston, Robert W. *Witch, Wicce, Mother Goose*, Harlow, Middlesex: Longman, 2001

Watson, Godfrey. *Bothwell and the Witches*, London: Robert Hale, 1975

Wilby, Emma. *Cunning Folk and Familiar Spirits: Shamanistic Visionary Traditions in Early Modern British Witchcraft and Magic*, Sussex Academic Press, 2005

WEBSITES

Listed here is just a tiny selection of websites currently providing further information on the topics covered in this Brief History. Some of the sites cover general medieval history and primary source materials whilst others are dedicated specifically to the history of witchcraft.

http://www.witchtrials.co.uk/
http://www.nationalgeographic.com/features/97/salem/
http://www.fordham.edu/halsall/sbook.html
http://www.georgetown.edu/labyrinth/
http://www.malleusmaleficarum.org/
http://www.templarhistory.com/
http://gethelp.library.upenn.edu/guides/hist/witchcraft.html
http://www.histarch.uiuc.edu/harper/religlink.html
http://www.shc.ed.ac.uk/Research/witches/index.html

INDEX